W9-AGY-580

The Trouble with Friendship

The Trouble with Friendship

Why Americans Can't Think Straight About Race

Benjamin DeMott

Yale University Press
New Haven and London

Published 1995 by Atlantic Monthly Press
Reprinted 1998 by Yale University Press by arrangement with
Grove/Atlantic, Inc.

Copyright © 1995 by Benjamin DeMott

Portions of Chapters 1 and 2 appeared in *Harper's Magazine*,
September 1995, under the title "Masking the Difference Between
Blacks and Whites."

All rights reserved.
This book may not be reproduced, in whole or in part, including
illustrations, in any form (beyond that copying permitted by Sections
107 and 108 of the U.S. Copyright Law and except by reviewers for
the public press), without written permission from the publishers.

Printed in the United States of America by Vail-Ballou Press,
Binghamton, New York.

Library of Congress Cataloging-in-Publication Data

DeMott, Benjamin, 1924–
      The trouble with friendship : why Americans can't think
straight about race / Benjamin DeMott.
            p. cm.
Originally published: 1st ed. New York : Atlantic Monthly Press.
c1995.
      Includes bibliographical references.
      ISBN 0-300-07394-1 (pbk. : alk. paper)
      1. United States—Race relations. I. Title.
[E185.615.D46 1998]
305.8'00973—dc21   97-50279
                              CIP

A catalogue record for this book is available from the British Library.

The paper in this book meets the guidelines for permanence and
durability of the Committee on Production Guidelines for Book
Longevity of the Council on Library Resources.

10 9 8 7 6 5 4 3 2 1

For Tom and Benj,

with love

Contents

Contents

Introduction

This book is about some remarkable yet unrecognized new stances that American blacks and whites are taking toward each other—new behaviors, new attitudes, new thinking. Closely connected with the national turn to the right, the new thinking is reflected in current public policy on welfare and many related matters. It appears to be causing a major schism among African American leaders. And it's everywhere in popular culture, shaping the stories that teach the races how to think about each other.

The reasons that the attitudes and ideas in question

have gone unrecognized, as political and cultural forces, are worth exploring, and the pages ahead offer some explanations. But I'm mainly concerned with description. What is the content of the new themes, how are they related to one another, how exactly do they function? What are their probable long-term consequences for society as a whole? These are this book's principal subjects.

One commonplace in the new thinking is criticism of "coddling." Liberal activists of both races are attacked for fostering an enfeebling psychology of dependency that discourages African Americans from committing themselves to individual self-development. This charge was passionately voiced by Shelby Steele in *The Content of Our Character* (1990), a work that attributes the difference between black rates of advance and those of other minority groups to government pampering. Most blacks, Steele claims, could make it on their own—as Italians, Irish, and Jews have done, and as Koreans and Southeast Asians are currently doing—were they not held back by devitalizing dogmas (and accompanying white-sponsored "programs") that present them, to themselves and others, as somehow dissimilar to and weaker than other Americans.

It's a divisive argument, rejected by many leaders for whom the Civil Rights era was formative. Jesse Jackson continues to call for new federal intervention on the side of the minority, John E. Jacob advocates "a Marshall Plan for the cities," and Henry Louis Gates combines his calls for "individual responsibility" with insistence that the country "take [black] people off welfare and train them for occupations relevant to a twenty-first century economy." Furious demands for "reparations" are still heard. Recent all-black panel discussions like those printed in *The New York Times Magazine* and the *Boston Review* and aired on PBS news shows reverberate with accusation and counteraccusation. Nevertheless the message comes across, winning widespread support: blacks should suspect aid from "outside," should realize that demands for such aid no longer bespeak strength; they must grasp that, in the market society, freedom lies not in group special interest bargaining but in self-made individualistic success—that which alone establishes the essential equality of blacks and all other Americans.

Tightly related to the indictment of alleged coddling is the theme of black-white equality and sameness—a theme central in the new thinking. For some time the language of sameness has been regularly summoned at hours of crisis: riots, burning, explosions of rage. Functioning as a social balm or salve, it assures the community that these virulent outbreaks can be coped with—that practical means of coping are immediately available. The basic assertion is that to achieve peace and harmony whites and blacks must work toward recognition of their fundamental commonality, must undertake, as individuals, to see through superficial differences to the needs and longings that all share. The discourse declares that we must teach ourselves how to get along together and how to become friends. We must—in the words of the Garth Brooks tune—learn to ignore "the color of skin" and "look for . . . the beauty within." Public officials take the lead in voicing this message, and their words are echoed by corporate executives, academic leaders, pundits, popular entertainers—even on occasion by black and white victims of racist beatings.

The theme of interracial identity-under-the-skin amounts to more, though, than a mere pacifier useful in periods of crisis. It has become a critical element of the same mind-set in which antipathy to "dependency" finds a place. Through its ubiquity in an extraordinary range of media, it seems, indeed, to be fashioning a new secular orthodoxy: the friendship orthodoxy of our time.

Understanding the ways of thought that coalesce in this orthodoxy calls for scrutiny of cultural materials of many sorts—political oratory, editorials, columns, commercials, movies, and much besides. It also requires alertness to substantive socioeconomic trends—because the ideas and symbols that focus the thinking are inseparable from happenings in the worlds of money, jobs, careers. The indictment of the dependency syndrome and coddling, for instance, could not have secured an audience before civil rights guarantees were in place and blacks began winning prominence in urban politics, elite education, and elsewhere. (The existence, in number, of self-sustaining, gainfully employed, up-wardly mobile blacks provided backing for the argu-ment that African American need for outside aid was overstated.) The same holds for the theme of black-white identity-under-the-skin. That theme has earned majority culture favor partly because several million blacks now work—and lunch and gossip—side by side with whites in venues where they can be seen by whites as "just like us," and from which, barely a generation ago, they were excluded.

The assumptions studied in this book mirror, in short, both the turn from liberalism to conservatism and broad changes in patterns of daily human activity—earning, spending, work, play; the assumptions and the cultural materials embodying them are signs of historic transformations in progress. The real-world event con-ditioning all the attitudes I examine is the emergence of a black middle class.

Political agendas routinely figure in references to the "moving up" black population—its size, composition, background, and rate of expansion. And it follows that political agendas exert strong influence on the new thinking that I call "friendship orthodoxy." Putting the same point differently: the relation between perceived minority affluence and the new thinking is mediated, and the mediators have procured a measure of auton-omy. The voice of friendship orthodoxy has exceptional range; it draws together liberals, conservatives, and centrists; it pronounces on all manner of subjects, from the history of black-white relations to the causes of contemporary race tension.

And—the reason for this book—its pronouncements with few exceptions tend to muddle, not clarify, race realities. Disputing whether the right or the left gains more from the confusion serves no purpose; the sensible project is working to end the confusion—trying to correct the increasingly destructive misjudgments and delusions about where, in regard to race, this country has been, presently stands, and is headed. I believe that, to achieve interracial harmony and continued black advance, blacks and whites alike need to reawaken to the complexity of the issues that the new enlightened mindset badly oversimplifies. My book aims to speed that reawakening.

Chapter 1

Visions of Black-White Friendship

At the heart of today's thinking about race lies one relatively simple idea: the race situation in America is governed by the state of personal relations between blacks and whites. Belief in the importance of personal relations reflects traits of national character such as gregariousness, openness, down-to-earthness. It also reflects American confidence that disputes can be trusted to resolve themselves if the parties consent to sit down together in the spirit of good fellowship— break bread, talk things out, learn what makes the other side tick.

But there's rather more to faith in black-white friendship than off-the-rack Rotarianism. There are convictions about the underlying sameness of black and white ways of thinking and valuing, and about the fundamental causes of racial inequity and injustice, and about the reasons why the idea of addressing race problems through political or governmental moves belongs to time past.

One leading assumption is that blacks and whites think and feel similarly because of their common humanity. (Right responsiveness to racial otherness and full access to black experience therefore require of whites only that they listen attentively to their inner voice.) Another assumption is that differences of power and status between whites and blacks flow from personal animosity between the races—from "racism" as traditionally defined. (White friendship and sympathy for blacks therefore diminishes power differentials as well as ill feeling, helping to produce equality.) Still another assumption is that bureaucratic initiatives meant to "help" blacks merely prolong the influence of yesteryear. (The advent of good interpersonal feeling between blacks and whites, on the other hand, lessens yesteryear's dependency.)

Each of these closely related assumptions surfaces regularly in print media treatment of the friendship theme—material promoting interracial amity and weaving together concern for "the disadvantaged" and the "underclass," anecdotal evidence of the mutual affection of blacks and whites, and implicit or explicit disparagement of politics and politicians. And traces of the same assumptions appear in fraternal gestures favored by campaigning political candidates.

White candidates attend services at black churches, socialize at black colleges, play games with blacks (as when, during Campaign '92, Jerry Brown took gang leaders rafting). And candidates speak out in favor of black-white friendships, venturing that such ties could be the answer to race riots. On the second day of the Los Angeles riots, Candidate Clinton declared: "White Americans are gripped by the isolation of their own experience. Too many still simply have no friends of other races and do not know any differently."

But fantasies about black-white friendship are dramatized most compellingly for large audiences in images. Movies, TV, and ads spare us abstract generalizing about the isolation of the races. They're funny and breezy. At times, as in *Natural Born Killers*, they deliver the news of friendship and sympathy in contexts of violence and amorality. At times they deliver that news through happy faces, loving gestures, memorable one-liners. Tom Hanks as Forrest Gump loses his beloved best buddy, a black (Mykelti Williamson), in combat and thereafter devotes years to honoring a pledge made to the departed (*Forrest Gump*, 1994). A rich white lady (Jessica Tandy) turns to her poor black chauffeur (Morgan Freeman) and declares touchingly: "Hoke, you're my best friend" (*Driving Miss Daisy*,

1989). Michael Jackson pours his heart into a race-dismissing refrain: "It doan matter if you're black or white" (1991). Scene and action hammer home the message of interracial sameness; mass audiences *see* individuals of different color behaving identically, sometimes looking alike, almost invariably discovering, through one-on-one encounter, that they need or delight in or love each other.

Item: The black actor Danny Glover sits on the john in *Lethal Weapon*, trousers around his ankles, unaware of a bomb ticking in the bowl; Danny's white buddy, Mel Gibson, breezily at home in Danny's house, saves his life by springing him from the throne to the tub.

Item: A commercial set in a gym finds two jock-side-kicks, one black, one white—Kareem Abdul-Jabbar and Larry Bird—chummily chaffing each other. Kareem bets Larry that he can't eat just one Lay's potato chip. The little devils are too tasty. Kareem wins the bet and the old cronies exit together, clever camera work and a makeup cap on Larry's head redoing them into interchangeable, dome-headed twins.

Item: The Tonight Show re-creates itself in the image of interracial bonhomie, replacing a white band with a black band, encouraging chat between white host and black second banana music director, and casually alluding to hitherto unpublicized black-white associations. (Jay Leno to Branford Marsalis: "I toured with Miles Davis.")

Item: Pulp Fiction (1994) draws together three sickeningly violent narratives by means of an overarching theme of sacrifice—blacks and whites risking all for each other. At the pivotal crisis, luck offers a white, mob-doomed prizefighter (Bruce Willis) a chance to escape; the black mobster (Ving Rhames) who's after him, is himself entrapped—raped and tortured, within Willis's hearing, by two white perverts. Spurning self-interest, Willis risks his life and saves the mobster. (The rescued black closes the racial gap in a phrase: "There's no more you and me.")

A key, early contribution to the mythology of black-white friendship was that of *The Cosby Show.* Without actually portraying blacks and whites interacting, and without preaching directly on the subject, this sitcom lent strong support to the view that white friendship and sympathy could create sameness, equality, and interchangeability between the races. Under the show's aegis an unwritten, unspoken, *felt* understanding came alive, buffering the force both of black bitterness and resentment toward whites and of white bitterness and resentment toward blacks. *Race problems belong to the passing moment. Race problems do not involve group interests and conflicts developed over centuries.*

Benjamin DeMott

Race problems are being smoothed into nothingness, gradually, inexorably, by goodwill, affection, points of light.

The Cosby family's cheerful at-homeness in the lives of the comfortably placed middle class, together with the fond loyalty of their huge audience, confirmed both the healing power of fellow feeling and the nation's presumably irreversible evolution—as blacks rise from the socioeconomic bottom through the working poor to the middle class—toward color blindness. In the years before the show, black-white themes, in film as well as TV, had passed through several stages of development. One of a half-dozen milestones was the introduction, in *The Jeffersons,* of the first blacks to achieve middle-class affluence via entrepreneurship. Another milestone was the introduction, by adoption, of charming black children into white families—as in *Webster* and *Diff'-rent Strokes.* (The "white foster parents," wrote Jannette Dates, "could then socialize the youngsters into the 'real' American way.")

And in the wake of the success of *The Cosby Show,* the eradication of race difference by friendship became an ever more familiar on-camera subject. Closeness between the races ceased to be a phenomenon registered indirectly, in surveys documenting the positive reaction of white audiences to the Huxtables; it moved to the center of mass entertainment. Everywhere in the visual media, black and white friendship in the here and now was seen erasing the color line. Interracial intimacy became a staple of mass entertainment story structures.*

Consider *White Men Can't Jump* (1992), a movie about a white quester—a dropout eking a living on basketball courts in Los Angeles—surviving, with black help, on ghetto turf. Working first as a solitary, the young white hustles black ballplayers on their own turf,

---

*A monograph on these structures in the movies would reach back to breakthrough works such as *The Defiant Ones, Brian's Song, Guess Who's Coming to Dinner,* and *Hurry Sundown.* Some notion of the quantity of relevant recent "product" can be gained from a more or less random list of recent films—TV and junk action movies mingling with more pretentious work—that treat race friendship themes for part or the whole of their length: *The Shawshank Redemption, Lethal Weapon I–III, The Waterdance, Ghost, The Last Boy Scout, 48 Hrs. I–II, Rising Sun, Iron Eagle I–II, Rudy, Above the Law, Sister Act I–II, Heart of Dixie, Betrayed, The Power of One, Crossroads, White Nights, Clara's Heart, Storyville, Clean and Sober, Doc Hollywood, Cool Runnings, Places in the Heart, Grand Canyon, Trading Places, Gardens of Stone, The Saint of Fort Washington, Dutch, Fried Green Tomatoes, Q & A, Passenger 57, Skin Game, That Was Then . . . This Is Now, Platoon, The Last Outlaw, A Mother's Courage: The Mary Thomas Story, Off Limits, The Unforgiven, The Air Up There, Cop and a Half, Made in America, The Pelican Brief, Losing Isaiah, Corrina, Corrina, Tyson, Everybody's All American, The Little Princess, Diehard with a Vengeance, Angels in the Outfield, Samaritan: The Mitch Snyder Story, Searching for Bobby Fischer, Soapdish, Homer and Eddie, Running Scared, Little Nikita, The Stand, An Officer and a Gentleman, American Clock, Yanks, State of Emergency, Poltergeist, Dr. Detroit, P.C.U., Flight of the Intruder, Ghostbusters, Lionheart, The Blues Brothers, Prayer of the Rollerboys, The Client, The Abyss, Showdown, Robin Hood: Men in Tights, A Matter of Justice, Smoke, Under Siege II, Clueless,* and so on.

trading insults with blacks far more powerful, physically, than himself. He chides black athletes to their faces for being showboats, concerned about looking good, not about winning. He flashes rolls of bills and is never mugged. Accompanied only by his girlfriend, he walks the most dangerous ghetto streets at night, once making his way uninvited into an apartment filled with black ballplayers. He mocks black musical performers to their faces in a park, describing the hymns they sing as "shit." That an arrogant, aggressive, white wiseass can do all this and more and emerge unscathed means partly that his behavior is protected under the laws of comedy.

But the armor that counts more, here as in numberless black-white friendship tales, is provided by the black buddy. The acquaintance of white Billy Hoyle (Woody Harrelson) and black Sidney Deane (Wesley Snipes) begins badly: each hoaxes the other. Later they communicate through taunts. Black taunts white for incapacity to appreciate the black musicians whom white claims to admire. "Sure, you can listen to Jimi [Hendrix]. Just, you'll never hear him." Black taunts white for dreaming that he can slam-dunk: "White men can't jump." Black mockingly offers technical aid to white: pumping up his Air Jordans for dream-flight. White jabs back hard, charging black with exhibitionism and sex obsession.

Yet the two make it as friends, form a team, work their scams in harmony. More than once the buddies save each other's tails, as when a black ballplayer whom they cheat turns violent, threatening to gun them down. (The two make a screaming getaway in the white quester's vintage ragtop.) And the movie's climax fulfills the equation—through sympathy to sameness and interchangeability. During a citywide, high-stakes, two-on-two tournament, Billy, flying above the hoop like a stereotypical black player, scores the winning basket on an alley-oop from his black chum, whereupon the races fall into each other's arms in yelping, mutual, embracing joy. Cut to the finale that seals the theme of mutual need and interdependency; black Sidney agrees to find quasi-honest work for white Billy at the floor-covering "store" that he manages:

BILLY (helpless): I gotta get a job. Can you give me a job?
SIDNEY (affectionately teasing): Got any references?
BILLY (shy grin): You.

Like many if not most mass entertainments, *White Men Can't Jump* is a vehicle of wish fulfillment. What's wished for and gained is a land where whites are unafraid of blacks, where blacks ask for and need nothing from whites (whites are the needy ones; blacks generously provide them with jobs), and where the revealed sameness of the races creates shared ecstatic highs. The precise details of the dream matter less than the force that makes it come true for both races, eliminating the constraints of objective reality and redistributing resources, status, and capabilities. That force is remote from political and economic policy and reform; it is, quite simply, personal friendship.

Another pop breeding ground of delusion is the story structure that pairs rich whites and poor blacks in friendship—as in *Regarding Henry* (1991), a Mike Nichols film about a white corporation lawyer and a black physical therapist. The two men meet following a holdup during which a gunman's stray bullet wounds the lawyer, Henry Turner (Harrison Ford), in the head, causing loss of speech, memory, and physical coordination. The therapist, Bradley (Bill Nunn), labors successfully at recovering Henry's faculties.

In outline, *Regarding Henry*—a video store hit—is a tale of moral transformation. Henry Turner is a corporate Scrooge who earns a fortune defending insurance companies against just suits brought by the injured and impecunious. Between the time of the gunshot wound and his return to his law firm, he experiences a change of heart—awakens to the meanness and corruption of his legal work and begins a movement toward personal reform. The sole influence on this transformation is Bradley, who shows the lawyer a persuasive example of selfless concern for others.

Bradley is called upon, subsequently, to give further guidance. Back in his luxo apartment and offices, Henry

Turner, aware finally of the amoral selfishness of his professional life and of his behavior as husband and father, sags into depression—refuses to leave his bed. His wife, Sarah (Annette Bening), summons the black therapist, the only man Henry respects. Over beer in Henry's kitchen, Bradley tells his host of a crisis of his own—a football injury which, although it ended his athletic career, opened the prospect of the more rewarding life of service he now leads.

But does Bradley really believe, asks Henry Turner, that he's better off because of the accident? His black friend answers by citing the satisfactions of helping others, adding that, except for his football mishap, "I would never have gotten to know you."

The black man speaks as though fully convinced that his own turning point—his unwanted second choice of life—and Henry Turner's are precisely similar. Nothing in his voice hints at awareness either of the gap between riches and privation or of the ridiculousness of the pretense that race and class—differences in inherited property, competencies, beliefs, manners, advantages, burdens—don't count. Wealthy white lawyer and humble black therapist speak and behave as though both were Ivy League clubmen, equally knowledgeable about each other's routines, habits, tastes. The root of Bradley's happiness as he sings his song of praise to his white buddy is that, for Henry Turner, difference doesn't exist.

The predictable closer: a new Henry Turner launches an effort at restitution to the poor whom his chicanery has cheated; black-white friendship not only makes us one but makes us good.

When crime enters, fellow feeling should in theory exit. But visions of the force of friendship challenge this rule, too. They thrust characters and audiences into hitherto unexplored passages of self-interrogation and self-definition, obliging whites to clarify, for themselves, the distinction between humane and racist responses to troubling black behavior. And they present the process of arriving at a humane response—i.e., one that doesn't allow a criminal act to derail black-white sympathy and friendship—as an act of personal reparation.

As in John Guare's highly praised *Six Degrees of Separation* (1990; movie version 1993). This work alludes to a real-life episode involving the victimization of a Manhattan family by a young black hustler, and it develops two themes. The first is that of black hunger for white friendship. The second is that of white readiness to suffer any injury if doing so is the only means of maintaining a one-on-one experience of sympathy and sameness with the other race.

Like Bradley the therapist, Paul, the hustler in the story, poses no black counterview—at the level of beliefs, tastes, feelings, or aspirations—to the values of rich whites. A man without a history, he studies and apes white, upper-bourgeois manners—speech, accents, clothes—not for the purpose of better cheating his models but out of desire to make those manners his own. When the heroine he's hustling asks him, "What did you want from us?" he answers, honestly, "Everlasting friendship." He tells her husband, an art dealer, "What I should do is what you do—in art but making money out of art and meeting people and not working in an office."

He begs the couple to "let me stay with you," tells them, again truthfully, that an evening he spent with them—before his scam was discovered—was "the happiest night I ever had." The heroine sums it up: "He wanted to be us. Everything we are in the world, this paltry thing—our life—he wanted it. He stabbed himself to get in here. He envied us."

This black idolater of fashionable white "grace," "style," and "tolerance"—this youngster obsessed with being one of *them*—defines the world as the majority might wish it: a place wherein the agency of interracial friendship can create, in itself, with minimum inconvenience, conditions of relative sameness between blacks and whites. And the relationship between Paul and the heroine dramatizes the imagined eagerness of whites—once they as individuals discover the rewards of one-on-one friendship—to go to any limit to preserve and nourish the friendship.

The heroine seldom wavers in her determination to indemnify the hustler for the injuries he does her. She knows the man to be a liar, knows him to be a thief, knows he's caused an innocent man's suicide and has betrayed her husband. Beyond all this she knows that, although her attachment to him is moral-imaginative, not sexual (the hustler is a homosexual), it's endangering her marriage.

Yet, in keeping with the overarching vision (sympathy heals all), she denies him nothing—not understanding, not kindness, not the goods of her house. Word that he may have killed himself brings her to the edge of hysteria. And at the crisis of the work her forbearance is dramatized as joy. The hustler, wanted for thievery, agrees to turn himself in to the police—and at once begins interrogating his white friend and victim about what she'll do to ease his imprisonment. Will she write to him when he's in jail? Yes, she promises. Will she send him books and tapes? Yes again. Will she visit him in jail? Yes. Will she wear her best clothes on these visits? "I'll knock them dead."

As her pledges come faster and more freely, the pace of the hustler's importunacy quickens; he pushes her— his victim-friend—harder, ever harder, as though intent on driving her to the borders of her generosity, the far reaches of her sufferance. His demands carry no hint of racewide protest at general injustice, no suggestion of any motive except that of one individual black's personal longing for the unconditioned, unconstrained friendship of whites.

Will they—the white woman and her husband— help him find work when he's out? Will they let him work for them, learn from them, learn the whole trade of art dealing, "not just the grotty part"? "Top to bottom" is the answer. The scene mounts to a climax at which the white woman's exuberant realization that her generosity has no limits tears a burst of wild laughter from the center of her being:

PAUL: You'll help me find a place?

OUISA: We'll help you find a place.

PAUL: I have no furniture.

OUISA: We'll help you out.

PAUL: I made a list of things I liked in the museum.
    Philadelphia Chippendale.

OUISA (bursts out laughing): Believe it or not, we have
    two Philadelphia Chippendale chairs—

PAUL: I'd rather have one nice piece than a room full of
    junk.

OUISA: Quality. Always. You'll have all that.
    Philadelphia Chippendale.

You'll have all that: a personal covenant, a lone white woman's guarantee, to a black hustler, that she'll sacrifice endlessly to ensure his well-being. Audiences are bound into that covenant by the final blackout, identifying with the passionate sacrament of the heroine's pledges, vicariously sharing the ideal of self-abnegating beneficence to black countrymen who long to become their friends. At its climax *Six Degrees of Separation* is about the "truth" that individual whites and blacks can scarcely bear not being each other. And the play's lesson is twofold: first, when whites are drawn into friendship and sympathy, one on one, with blacks, they will go to extreme lengths to suppress vexations and the sense of injury; second, once blacks are awarded unconditional white friendship, *as individuals*, they cease to harbor any sense of vexation or injury that would need suppressing.

The message confirms, for the right-minded majority, that racism is one-dimensional—lacking, that is, in institutional, historical, or political ramifications. And the quantity of similar confirmation elsewhere in popular entertainment is, speaking matter-of-factly, immense.

Incessantly and deliberately, the world of pop is engaged in demonstrating, through images, that racism has to do with private attitudes and emotions—with personal narrowness and meanness—not with differences in rates of black and white joblessness and poverty, or in black and white income levels, or in levels of financing of predominantly black and white public schools. The images body forth an America wherein some are more prosperous than others but all—blacks as well as whites—rest firmly in the "middle income sector" (the rising black middle class encompasses all blacks), where the free exchange of kindness should be the rule.

This America is of course remote from fact. One out of every two black children lives below the poverty line (as compared with one out of seven white children).

Nearly four times as many black families exist below the poverty line as white families. Over 60 percent of African Americans have incomes below $25,000. For the past thirty years black unemployment rates have averaged two to three times higher than those of whites.

But in the world of pop, racism and fraternity have to do solely with the conditions of personal feeling. Racism is unconnected with ghetto life patterns that abstractions such as income and employment numbers can't dramatize. Racism has nothing to do with the survival strategies prudently adopted by human beings without jobs or experience of jobs or hope of jobs. It has no link with the rational rejection, by as many as half the young black men in urban America, of such dominant culture values as ambition, industry, and respect for constituted authority. Pop shows its audiences that racism is *nothing but* personal hatred, and that when hatred ends, racism ends. The sweet, holiday news is that, since hatred is over, we—blacks and whites together, knit close in middleness—have already overcome.

Chapter 2

The Mystique of Sympathy

The themes of the stories that dominate mass entertainment match the lines of argument put forth soberly by opinion makers who are perceived as thoughtful, discerning, and authoritative. Simplified, sanitized versions of the race problem can't be escaped, in short, merely by turning off the tube. Narrative-dramatic forms that aspire to amuse strip experience of its social context, and delete history and politics; their focus is upon the course of personal relationships between particular blacks and particular whites. Expository forms that aspire to educate function differently. Instead of

deleting social contexts, they allude to them for the purpose of discounting them, suggesting that social influences on individual lives have been exaggerated and
arguing that friendship is indeed the master key to
peace, harmony, and justice. That notion is advanced
with a reasoned air—no music, color, comedy, or dramatic tension. But only in these respects is it incompati-
ble with the race message developed in pop.

It's not unusual, in fact, for writers trusted as
spokespersons for serious humane opinion to offer specific proposals designed to increase the flow of friendli-
ness between the races. In his recent book *Race* (1992),
Studs Terkel proposes that what America needs, to ease
race relations, is a mode of behavior he calls "affirmative civility."

> As I walk down the street . . . I see an elderly
> black woman, toting two heavy bags. She's fin-
> ished a day's work at the white lady's house. She is
> weary, frowning. I say, as a matter of course,
> "How's it goin'?" Her face brightens. "Fine. And
> you?"
>
> Three young black kids are swaggering along.
> As they come toward me, I say, "How's it goin'?"
> The tall one in the middle is startled. "Fine. And
> you?"
>
> A presence was acknowledged. That was all.
>
> I am not suggesting a twilight stroll through
> . . . a public housing project. The danger is not so

much black hostility as a stray bullet fired by one black kid at another. What I am suggesting is something else: Affirmative Civility.

Terkel's thinking, like that of many white liberals, runs roughly thus: the rights and wrongs of race are obvious; depending on the state of our inner feelings, we're either part of the problem or part of the solution. We're part of the solution if we have the courage to break out of the prison of our skin color and say hello, as equals, one-on-one, to black strangers . . . if we have a touch of imagination about the way an elderly black person might feel at the end of her workday . . . if we're shrewd enough to realize that although urban life poses dangers, the sparky gestures of black youngsters approaching on the sidewalk aren't necessarily a mortal threat.

We're part of the problem, on the other hand, if we have an aversion to black people or are frightened of them, or if we feel that the more distance we put between them and us the better, or if we're in the habit of asserting our superiority rather than acknowledging the humanity we share.

Granted, the argument goes, too much optimism is foolish. But we need to begin somewhere. The central elements of the problem of race are the strains of suspicion and fear found within the white heart; solving the problem demands that we work on ourselves, seeking to transform chilly, dark detachment into warm, fraternal feeling.

This approach, like that of pop narratives, miniaturizes, personalizes, and moralizes the large and complex dilemmas of race, removing them from the public sphere. History and social forces seem more or less beside the point, feelings become decisive, and the fate of black Americans is seen as shaped in no negligible part by events occurring in the hearts and minds of the privileged—art dealers, corporation lawyers, basketball hustlers, whomever—as they enter into one-on-one interracial encounter.

Not astonishingly, some who reflect earnestly on black-white personal relations discover that a quasi-religious or mystical dimension lies near the center of the subject. Their essays or columns carefully detail occasions when whites and blacks experience liberation from color, are set free from the distractions of race, and are allowed to live into the warmth of each other's humanity. Informally and unpretentiously they teach readers that black-white friendship creates not a comedic interchangeability (as in chuckling commercials and sports movies), but a deep soul-connectedness.

An example: In a 1992 *Family Circle* column called "Carefully Taught," TV's Roger Rosenblatt dwells on the parental obligation to teach children not to hate. He explains his special personal concern with prejudice (because he's Jewish, his wife's Episcopalian parents opposed their daughter's marriage to him). And he includes an account of the methods he and his wife employ in fighting "categorical hatred" in their home. The couple denounces stereotypes at their first eruption: "One day our daughter, Amy, then six, wondered aloud if a delivery boy was inept because he was black. We came down on her hard—much too hard, given her age and the size of the incident. But Amy got the point." Urging others to take on the task of stamping out racism in the home, Rosenblatt self-deprecatingly praises his own and his wife's commitment to fairness: "This is one right thing we have done as parents. In the reverse of the song from *South Pacific*, we have carefully taught all our children not to hate."

The main lesson of "Carefully Taught," however, is that white friendship and sympathy for blacks not only make power differentials vanish but create a kind of spiritual identity between us, one by one. The lesson is drawn from an episode which reveals, more or less incidentally, the personal sensitivity, to injured blacks, of one of the Rosenblatt children.

"When our oldest child, Carl, was in high school," Rosenblatt writes, "he and two black friends were standing on a street corner in New York City one spring evening, trying to hail a taxi. The three boys were dressed decently and were doing nothing wild or threatening. Still, no taxi would pick them up. If a driver spotted Carl first, he might slow down, but he would take off again when he saw the others. Carl's two companions were familiar with this sort of abuse. Carl, who had never observed it firsthand before, burned with anger and embarrassment that he was the color of a world that would so mistreat his friends."

Rosenblatt notes that when his son "was applying to colleges, he wrote his essay on that taxi incident with his two black friends. . . . He was able to articulate what he could not say at the time—how ashamed and impotent he felt. He also wrote of the power of their friendship, which has lasted to this day and has carried all three young men into the country that belongs to them. To all of us."

In this piece of writing white sympathy begets interracial sameness in several distinct ways. The three classmates are said to react identically to the cabdriver's snub: i.e., they feel humiliated. "[Carl] could not find the words to express his humiliation and his friends *would* not express theirs."

The anger that inspires the younger Rosenblatt's college admissions essay on racism is seen as identical with black anger. Friendship brings the classmates together as joint, equal owners of the land of their birth ("the country that belongs to [all of] them"). And a still larger vision of essential black-white sameness is supplied by the author near the end: "Our proper hearts tell the truth," he declares, "which is that we are all in the same boat, rich and poor, black and white. We are helpless, wicked, heroic, terrified, and we need one another. We need to give rides to one another."

The will to aggregate—to see blacks and whites as

"all in the same boat"—strengthens as more formerly pure-white institutions strive toward color blindness—and, of course, as more blacks attain middle-income status. In 1970 only 7 percent of African American families had incomes above $50,000; over the next twenty years the figure rose to 14 percent. In the same period scholarship opportunities for blacks at elite schools and colleges greatly expanded. White parents of children attending expensive private schools meet black parents at school meetings and elsewhere; they're moved toward a relaxed sense of black-white interchangeability by car pools and uniforms and conversation with their children's black chums over shared meals and weekends. A diminished sense of race barriers is, in these circumstances, natural.

Still: black infants die in America at twice the rate of white infants. Among black youths under age twenty, death by murder occurs nearly ten times as often as among whites. Over the past three decades the number of blacks in their early twenties with no earnings whatever has averaged three to four times higher than that of whites. Over half of the country's black mothers have never been married; over half of the country's black children live in single-parent families. It matters that the number of black families earning above $50,000 doubled in the last generation; it also matters that 85 percent of black America earns well below that sum, and that the Census Bureau reports the net worth of the typical white household to be ten times that of the typical black household.

Broken out by race, indeed, social tabulations argue that most black parents continue to lack grounds for believing in their children's future—and that the majority of black sons and daughters continue to lack cause for valuing their own lives. The pleasing metaphors locating blacks and whites all in the same boat—equally able (because of friendship and sympathy) to do each other favors and "to give rides to one another"—replace real-life differentials.

And they also delete details of feeling that tend to clash with the message of interchangeability. In Rosenblatt's "Carefully Taught," taxi drivers' racist snubs are found to be similarly humiliating for sensitive whites and blacks—a stretched reading. (The pain of insults routinely suffered for generations and likely to continue into the future differs, surely, from the pain of a single insult observed with shock at a distance.)

The white father and the young blacks are found to take similar satisfaction in the younger Rosenblatt's breakthrough, in his admissions essay, to full expression of repugnance at racial injustice. And this too seems stretched. Blacks have long objected to being used, in morally self-aggrandizing ways, by whites engaged in presenting their own "character," reverence for principle, freedom from "prejudice," and the like.

Yet more questionable, perhaps, is the implicit finding, expressed in "we need one another," that a representative white's need for blacks resembles a representative black's need for whites. For the sympathetic white, need has the pleasant taste of discovered confraternity; not so, presumably, the taste of need as known by the majority of African Americans.

Differences like those passed over in "Carefully Taught," accumulating cell by cell, form the stuff of real-world race history. But the well-meaning consensus in pop and elsewhere makes light of difference, and shrugs off history and politics. Political action is mentionable, to be sure. "If we're looking for a formula to ease the tensions between the races," Rosenblatt observes, then we should "attack the disintegration of the black community" and "the desperation of the poor."

But that observation is alien to the temper of this mode of thought. The phrase "attack the disintegration" feels, in context, cold, abstract, a project for the lab; giving rides to one another feels immediate, warm, efficacious—akin to Studs Terkel's "How's it goin'?" Without overtly mocking formula hunters who look toward the political arena "to ease the tensions," "Carefully Taught" alludes to them in a throwaway tone conveying that practical, well-meaning whites look elsewhere. Because their class experience has closed, for them, the gap between the races, they listen to their proper hearts at moments of epiphany, and allow sympathy to work its magic.

* * *

Right-minded assertions that blacks and whites are all in the same boat ride, as I say, on a quasi-mystical undercurrent. And the chosen language often intimates that the creation of shared interracial realms of personal feeling represents spiritual advance—an achievement beyond those attainable by political means. There was a time for going to law—politicking for equal rights—but we've passed through it; there's a time in which the purer force of sympathy brings oneness into being, and that hour is near at hand.

John Updike improvises on this theme in "A Letter to My Grandsons" (1989). The novelist's elder daughter married a West African, and the couple has two sons, Kwame and Anoff; Updike's letter to the lads introducing them to their mother's family history is a richly loving document.

Like Rosenblatt, Updike alludes briefly to the facts of hatred. He tells his grandsons that "racial prejudice operates in the United States against blacks in many ways overt and oblique, and the black ghettos, as drugs surge and industrial jobs vanish, are perhaps more dire places than they ever were." But Updike's optimism matches Rosenblatt's, and he, too, nudges political action into the wings: "At least our laws now formally insist upon equal rights, and our best corporations and educational institutions recruit blacks in an effort to right old imbalances, and professional sports and television commercials constantly offer images of multiracial camaraderie. An ideal colorblind society flickers at the forward edge of the sluggishly evolving one."

Gently, Updike develops a notion of equal ownership paralleling that found in "Carefully Taught" ("the country that belongs to [all of us]"): "America is slowly becoming yours, I want to think, as much as it is anyone's."

And once more the foundation for this hope is felt to lie in the close communion of blacks and whites. Initially Updike stands at a distance, speaking as though he knew this communion only indirectly. He tells his grandsons that there's "a floating sexual curiosity and potential love [between the races] that in your parents has come to earth and borne fruit and that the blended shade of your dear brown skins will ever advertise." But as the phrase "your dear brown skins" suggests, the posture of detachment is soon dropped. In comely sentences, the "Letter" approaches its vision of black and white interchangeability via a touchstone in the author's own emotional life, a summit of "mutual ease and trust": "the moment the other evening when fretful little Kwame let himself be walked to sleep on my shoulder."

From this affecting image of a white elder comforting a black child the natural progress is toward minimization of the impact of race history on American society. Updike makes the move confidently. It's true, he acknowledges, that "you will each be in subtle (at best) ways the focus of distaste and hatred and fear that have nothing to do with anything but your skins." But, he insists, shutting the door briefly opened upon black-white difference, "we must all take our chances, and the world is not anywhere basically a friendly place, though our mothers and fathers and schoolteachers would make it seem so."

We are, in sum, all in the same boat. The chances of whites would seem appreciably better than those of blacks in, say, the state of Pennsylvania (where Updike was born), or Nebraska, or any other of the several states wherein *fifteen* times as many blacks as whites aged eighteen to thirty are in jail. But we must all take our chances.

The tone of "A Letter to My Grandsons" is a literary achievement. But, despite its delicacy, the "Letter" is a public document, and it is, like Studs Terkel's para-graphs advocating "affirmative civility," entirely repre-sentative of the new race thinking. The evolution of the ideal color-blind society is imagined to occur more within feelings than in response to policy change; the ideal society's origins lie not in the resolution of com-plex group conflict but in mysterious, irreversible move-ments of the passionate heart. Pasts disappear; individuals black and white find themselves taking even-money chances on level playing fields, giving (or not giving) each other rides (on each other's shoulders, or in cabs, or in getaway vintage ragtops) in accordance with personal impulse. Determined, molecular, exhausting effort by blacks to ensure that school success actually leads to better jobs, struggles to meet the educational needs of children in gang-terrorized projects—these warrant no special remark. It's assumed that *all* "our mothers and fathers and schoolteachers" labor to show their children that the world is "basically a friendly place"; it's not assumed that distinctions need to be drawn between parents whose imagination of a friendly world has been nurtured by rational expectations of decent jobs and decent wages and parents whose imagination of a friendly world has flickered only by the light of crack dreams.

Nor is it doubted that the experience of intimate white-black communion—the lived sense of interchangeability—can establish higher and lower orders of reality and time. Those caught up in this experience direct a mildly detached, Prospero-like gaze at the chaos of hostility and bestiality in the broader world. The apparent turbulence—the "problems"—is understood to be in some sense real; the political scene in some sense exists. But none of it feels substantive when compared with the pure moment of love. The new thinking and feeling melding in friendship orthodoxy prefers that moment to the endless, wearing cycles of conflict, confrontation, negotiation, ground gained, ground lost—the tenacity amidst frustration from which to this day "race progress" is wrung. The new orthodoxy charms and touches, and keeps social fact at bay.

*   *   *

The language of the orthodoxy isn't spoken solely by whites. (If that were the case, its power might well be reduced.) Among blacks of established place and achievement there are many who are taken by privatizing, historyless fantasies, enchanted by the mystique of sympathy. Articles in *Reconstruction*, Harvard's journal of contemporary black thought, often rhapsodize on moments of at-oneness between individual blacks and whites. James Alan McPherson lays it down in an essay that "the only possible steps, the safest steps . . . small ones" in the movement "toward a universal culture" will be those built on experiences of personal connectedness, not on "ideologies and formulas and programs." McPherson hears a black bag lady galvanize Grand Central Station with a song: "[She] turned her eyes upward toward the other world. . . . Her voice, or her conviction, was so powerful in that congested place that, mysteriously, her desperate optimism-in-despair caused a great number of cynical commuters to look up with her. For just one minute, there was a pause, and a silence, and a period of grace."

At another moment in his essay McPherson senses a field of sympathy between a young white woman and a black addict: "Just this past spring, when I was leaving a restaurant after taking a former student to dinner, a black [woman on the sidewalk] said to my friend, in a rasping voice, 'Hello, girlfriend. Have you got anything to spare?" The person speaking, it emerged, was a black female crack addict with a child who was also addicted. "But," says McPherson, when the addict made her pitch to his friend and dinner companion, "I saw in my friend's face an understanding and sympathy and a shining which transcended race and class. Her face reflected one human soul's connection with another. The magnetic field between the two women was charged with spiritual energy."

The path to progress, this writer argues, lies through interpersonal gestures by people who "insist on remaining human, and having human responses. . . . Perhaps the best that can be done, now, is the offering of understanding and support to the few out of many who are capable of such gestures, rather than devising another plan to engineer the many into one."

These Terkelian sentences constitute a more explicit address to the future of race politics than that found in many mainstream writers. The rhetoric is elevated and the state of mind wholly comprehensible. From the plateau of an evening of civilized social pleasure—giving dinner to a former student—the activist pushing, shoving, squeezing, coercing of yesteryear look coarse if not boorish; "engineer[ing] the many into one" feels mechanical, unnatural, and lowering. The writer's preference for the contemplative mode, his taste for the vocabulary of religion ("soul," "spiritual") is at once morally self-heightening and evasive. And, as it happens, counterparts to his impatience with "the ordinary dirty work of politics," as George Orwell termed it—to his impulse to turn away from the ten thousand items on the real-life agenda of activists for racial justice—are visible everywhere in the new race thought.

The attitudes in question have a background, for whites, worth careful regard. The community of well-meaning whites numbers many who, throughout their formative years, heard the language of race animus spoken by their own elders, in their own homes. For them the movement from race animus to affirmative civility and sympathy meant a break with the past—a serious advance from a negative to a positive. It destroyed modes of feeling that undergirded many types of narrow-mindedness, causing something conclusive and definitive to happen within family and class. (The Rosenblatt column itself recalls prohibitions against the intermarriage of Christian and Jew, as well as against friendship between whites and blacks.) The feelings of fulfillment and self-satisfaction accompanying the white achievement of "tolerance" help to explain not only the readiness to accept simplistic conceptions of racism (racism equals hatred; end hatred and you end racism) but also the mystical faith in the social power of sympathy; in addition, they explain the life-transforming sense of personal newness that finds expression in dismissals of history and politics.

The outlook shaped by this faith has some strengths and is only dimly understood, if at all, by baiters of political correctness who reject it as hypocritical or self-serving. Whites who press themselves to act "correctly" toward the minority are engaged in a significant, personal, moral project. Their behavior isn't simply a rejection of the meanness and contempt that were norms in the households of their youth; it's the justification of their refusal to assent to melodramatic claims that slavery never ended and progress never began. It gives them the right to dispute, on the basis of personal experience, agitators who insist blacks have scored no real advances in the past half century.

Witty mockers of PC (a minor subsection of friendship orthodoxy) completely ignore this truth—take no notice of the respects in which contemporary rules of speech represent an achievement. To its great credit, the new orthodoxy has established resistance to hatred as a defining element of the moral identity of reasoning people.

Yet the orthodoxy's defects clearly outweigh its strengths. Minds in its grip are poorly placed to defend themselves against reductive accounts either of racism or of black experience. Not by calculated intent but nevertheless with fearful consequences, they diminish historical catastrophes affecting millions over centuries, inflate the significance of relatively modest increments of socioeconomic progress, and overinterpret tremors of tenderness occurring within living individual hearts. Encouraging flights into sentimentality, they discourage patient address to the links between bad school performance now and little or no school availability for longer than a century, between negative social attitudes and still crushing levels of joblessness, between minority desperation and majority fear.

No less important: in confusing the manners of fraternity with the substance, the right-minded consensus tied to the new orthodoxy legitimizes wishful, preening self-deception.

Catching sight of an injury to blacks, I, a concerned white, experience disturbance, shame, and fellow feeling with the injured. But quickly a surge of self-approval—satisfaction in my sense of identification with the unlucky Other—sets things straight. *We must all take our chances.* It seems to me needless to ask how one white person's "sensitive" response can be helpful to the injured. It seems needless also to ask what public correctives are in course—what steps are being taken to ensure that tomorrow's white children will have fewer affecting stories of black injury and white sympathy to recite to their elders and to college admissions committees.

Issues of responsibility, plans for practical political change, reflection on the causes and meanings and dimensions of continuing injury—these seem irrelevancies. The seizing truth is that of the power of personal friendship and sympathy in the here and now. I salute the essential sameness of blacks and whites. *We must all take our chances. The society evolves. Wherever one looks one sees more well-off blacks.* My rhetoric effects a playful instant redistribution of life chances—of rights, property, risks. (The country that belongs to all of us.) As the political and socioeconomic mists clear, and the veil of apparent injury and pain parts, I glimpse the promise of happiness that "ideologies and formulas and programs" only obscure.

In sum, my orthodox, right-minded, self-congratulating way of thinking encourages me—a person of goodwill—to see through color. At small cost to myself, without negotiation, assured that my course and that of the thoughtful majority as a whole is right and generous, I erase the past and the dilemmas of power, and arrive at a still point where black and white are one.

Chapter 3

*Because
We Like Them:
A Sampler*

Today's mail brings a Wal-Mart flyer—a message from the nation's largest retailer, typical of advertising matter circulating nationally by the ton. In sidebars scattered among the specials, management speaks proudly of the quality of the general life of its workforce and of the quality of relationships between black and white employees. About Dell, the black manager of a snack bar who is pictured in a photo, management comments: "Before coming to Wal-Mart, Dell worked nights and was able to spend little or no time with her three children. Now, in addition to having more time for her children, she has a second family, her Wal-Mart Associates and Customers."

Everywhere illustrations dramatize fraternity within this second family. Black and white children hold hands. Boys' Fruit of the Loom separates are modeled, in an interracial two-shot, by "Travis, son of Gladys, Customer Service Manager," and "D.J., son of Denice, Departmental Manager." Boys' French Toast Swimwear features black "Joseph, son of Cecilia, Training Coordinator," and white "Jared, son of John, Assistant Manager." For Girls' Basic Tees it's white "Kaylyn, daughter of Janice, Electronics," and black "Tammy, daughter of Glenda, telephone operator"), and, among the grown-ups, Rachel, a black "Sales Associate," models misses swimwear beside white "Paula, wife of Terry, Manager," while Dell of the snack bar models Ladies' Plus Six woven tank tops in the company of white "Bobbie, Sales Associate."

Fun is the watchword. Joseph and Jared are at sand play, Kaylyn and Tammy chuckle delightedly at a babe in a bassinet, Dell and Bobbie are clearly old friends. In boxed quotations here and there employees black and white hail the "sense of family created when everyone is helping their customers and each other." They speak of an ineffable near-utopian atmosphere brought to life in this color-blind, posthatred, we-are-the-world corporate venue. "It's hard to describe," says John, assistant manager. "It is something you just have to see. I wouldn't want to be anywhere else."

* * *

An argument in linear prose by a John Updike or Roger Rosenblatt can tell us something about the terms on which "the race problem" is formally presented as personal and moral in nature—a matter of the feelings and attitudes of whites and blacks toward each other in present time. Films like *Regarding Henry*—stories that trace out stages in the development of personal friendship between representatives of the races—can show us why personalizing perspectives are perfectly adapted to commercially successful entertainment.

But scrutinizing texts one by one gives a false idea of the role of individual expression in supporting standardized enlightened opinion regarding black-white friendship, "race progress," and the rest. Friendship orthodoxy is maintained not by individual performers but by a nearly measureless quantity of cultural production, much of it as banal and repetitive and impersonal as a Wal-Mart flyer—material that for years has been continuously assembling and reassembling the basic elements of a single mode of thought. Well-meaning America awakens each morning to a minidramatization of black and white amity (Katie Couric nudging a perky elbow into good buddy Bryant Gumbel's side). It dozes off at midnight with cameras panning a largely white audience woofing for Arsenio Hall in syndication. At all hours of the day and night a black woman and a white woman (Dionne Warwick and Deborah Gregorian) can be seen companionably conversing, on behalf of the Psychic Friends Network, on the Prevue Channel. Mailboxes by the tens of millions are choked with outpourings from firms bent like Wal-Mart on publicizing both their social bona fides and their wares by displaying black and white models at cordial ease with each other. Blizzards of goodwill race images descend on the nation daily—space ad tributes, trumpetings of corporate largesse, commercials, sitcoms, news features, TV specials, masses of matter proclaiming that whites feel strongly positive impulses of friendship for blacks and that those impulses are effectively eradicating race differences, rendering blacks and whites the same.

A communications giant—AT&T—rents newspaper space to praise black soldiers "from the Revolutionary War to World War II to Desert Storm." Chrysler hails black naval heroes. Bank ads picture black entrepreneurial types smiling with pleasure at the assurance, in the accompanying copy, that "we'd like to be your bank for the life of your business" (Manufacturers Hanover). BellSouth TV commercials feature children singing, "I am the keeper of the world"—first a white child, then a black child, then a white child, then a black child.

We enjoy *them*, the undervoice murmurs. *Once it was otherwise, but today we* enjoy *them and like them and this makes us the same.*

Because Con Ed likes them, it announces a gift to New York's schoolchildren of book covers featur-

ing heroes and heroines of black history. Because
Coca-Cola cares, it announces a "Share-the-Dream
Sweepstakes" ($130,000 in scholarships for black
youngsters). Because Reebok cares, it's "encouraging
young athletes to be the best they can through our
neighborhood *Court Renewal Program.* We are refur-
bishing high-use, rundown playground courts all across
the country." Because Smucker's likes them, it's chosen
an African American father and son to introduce
Smucker's peach preserve as a low-calorie cereal sweet-
ener. Because Dow Chemical likes them, it's recruiting
young black college grads for its research division and
dramatizing, in TV commercials, their tearful-joyful
partings from home. ("Son, show 'em what you got,"
says a black lad's dad.) Because IBM likes them, it encourages staff to sign on as mentors ("with help from
teachers and school officials, [mentors] form close
bonds with individual students, meeting every week to
help with homework, to serve as role models, to advise
and to listen"). Because Brooklyn Union Gas likes them,
it avers—in a newspaper ad on Martin Luther King's
birthday—that "MLK has a very special place . . . in
our hearts." Because RJR Nabisco likes them, it ex-
horts readers—again on King's birthday—to "MAKE
EVERY DAY A DAY FOR MILK" (the ad proposes that
Dr. King's initials henceforth be understood to signify
"*M*ore *L*ove and *K*indness").

The clumsiness and saccharinity are immaterial.
What counts is the buildup—the repeated, vested, cul-

turally determined, self-validating gestures of friendship, the humming, buzzing background theme: *All decent Americans extend the hand of friendship to African
Americans; nothing but nothing is more auspicious for
the African American future than this extended hand.*

Sitcoms new or in rerun constantly group and re-
group the elements of sameness and sympathy orthodoxy. On *Designing Women* black and white
business partners (Anthony and Julia) reveal how sympathy and affection cause race differences to vanish in
the environs of Atlanta: On *Murphy Brown* Candice
Bergen comes to like and admire the new station manager—a black man who initially seemed threatening;
the two make common cause for "standards." On *Doo-
gie Howser, MD* the teenage medico hero is held hostage
in a drugstore holdup but makes friends with the teenage black hostage-taker, suggests the possibility of a
hospital job, and persuades his new hoodlum-friend to
release his hostages and turn himself in. On kiddie car-
toon shows jokes and gimmicks regularly highlight
black-white palship. (When Freddy Flintstone of *Flintstone Kids* takes a shot of friends with his Polarock
camera, a bespectacled black buddy is prominently
featured.)

Then there are the ad campaigns. American Express
focuses on an elegant black couple and an elegant white
couple seated together in a theater box, happy in each
other's company. (The couples share the box with an
oversized gold card.) Black Mom feeds miserably

coughing white Mom Robitussin in the TV commercial. Here's *People* magazine promoting itself under a full-bleed photo of John Lee Hooker, the black bluesman: "We're these kinds of people, too," *People* claims in the cutline. Here's an issue of *People* itself delighting, in the cover headline, that "Whoopi and Ted Are in Love."

LA Law follows a young black lawyer whose mother opposes his love affair with a white woman. "But, Mom," says the lawyer. "The reason I love her is that inside she's just like you." Jessica, the black woman lawyer on the CBS soap *As the World Turns*, marries white, debonair Duncan. On *Later* Camille Paglia compares herself with Anita Hill. A minor film called *The Super* explores the friendship of a white slumlord and a black youngster living in one of his buildings. A major film, *Philadelphia*, explores the friendship of two lawyers—white, AIDS-afflicted Tom Hanks and black, spiky Denzel Washington. (Hanks's mother, played by Joanne Woodward, underlines the black-white sameness theme: "I didn't raise my children," she says angrily, "to ride in the back of the bus.") Simi Valley and South Central Los Angeles field softball teams against each other in proof of mutual goodwill (CNN films the game). Black-white pop duets mount the charts—Aretha Franklin and George Michael, Conway Twitty and Brook Benton sharing choruses of "Rainy Night in Georgia." White talk show hosts, religious or sleazy, enjoy working with black sidekicks. On the *700 Club* Pat Robertson joshes Ben Kinchlow, his black sidekick, about Ben's far-out ties. (Pat's field companion is Mr. T.) On Jay Sekulow's courtroom show, *A Call to Action*, Jay is tight with his black field reporter, Ty Bragg. Ricki Lake's "Search for the Sexiest Man in America" features steamy leering by black and white contestants and judges with a cheering audience in the background. (Black judge, Roshumba, to white contestant: What sign would I see on your bedroom door? Contestant Chris, from Texas: Slippery when wet.) There's Rolanda, there's Oprah, there's the Fresh Prince, there's Montel . . .

Repeatedly, thanks to an army of sponsors, African Americans are presented as folks with whom the rest of America can identify—members of the regular-Joe, little-guy class—enemies of snobs, show-offs, wanna-bes. In adperson iconography blacks stand for *The People* and are indispensable in campaigns that market products by inventing and exploiting Us versus Them antipathies. Apple Computer launches a new little-guy/Big Brother battle against IBM by showing a professor inspiring an interracial computer classroom with talk of "a whole new era" in which "ordinary people" gain access to technology. ("The walls have come down! Opportunity has gone up!") The professor is black.

The tide of friendship images pulls the risky and dangerous into its current as well as the safe and easy. Heartened by the sense of fundamental black-white sameness, the enlightened teach themselves to respond fraternally to challenges posed by black aggression, hostility, even crime. *TV Guide* enfolds the fierce language of rap into playful good fellowship. "Check out this 'def' glossary," says the head above the magazine's feature intended to "help you speak the lingo." The lead reads: "Yo, G! Peep this." (A genteel white gloss is added: "May we have your attention, please?") The world of drive-by murder depicted in the movie *Boyz N the Hood* draws affirmative civility. A syndicated white columnist announces, after seeing the film, that he finds "the people [to be] attractive, likable types" and regrets that "few whites really know much about them."

A nonfiction genre thrives in which the central interest lies in the relationship between concerned white adults and black youngsters struggling to escape a life sentence in the projects. A pioneer contribution to the genre, Alex Kotlowitz's *There Are No Children Here* (1991), tells of the author's experience during two years spent hanging out with two young black brothers— "visiting them at home, accompanying them to school, playing basketball with them." (The writer and his subjects traveled the country together, promoting Kotlowitz's book and appearing on *The Oprah Winfrey Show* and numerous other programs.) Another major contribution to the genre, Darcy Frey's *The Last Shot* (1994), focuses on Frey's successful effort at building friendship and trust between himself and a group of young, talented, black basketball players—Coney Island school-

kids dreaming of pro careers. (The writer and his subjects grew so close that the latter entrusted him with
their jewelry and Walkmans while they played ball.)

Whole organizations are dedicated to fostering
friendship between white grown-ups and black children. William Bennett regularly celebrates Best Friends,
Inc., a Washington-based group founded by his wife
that specializes in developing direct, ongoing, one-on-
one, adult-child, interracial relationships.

Some Americans affect to believe that a near cult of
black-white friendship is in the making. "I'm not used
to black people," says the young hero of the successful
children's book *Lizard Music* on first meeting a black
grown-up who will become his best friend. "There are
only five black kids in our school and you never get a
chance to talk to them, because there is always a crowd
of kids around them showing how they're not prejudiced." The TV show host Bob Costas holds forth with a
guest—Pete Hamill, columnist—on this theme, arguing
that the culture is now sufficiently color blind to make it
needless for people constantly to feel they have to prove
they're well disposed toward blacks. On one view the
whole of the anti-PC movement qualifies as an expression of boredom with the pervasiveness of friendship
dogma.

And increasingly that boredom induces commentators—especially those employed by hip weeklies—to
devise new methods of enlivening the bonding of blacks
and whites. Criticizing a black rock singer's style, one

white *Village Voice* writer remarks that "the brother is confused." "Brother" belongs to the argot of black intraracial solidarity; the white writer confirms his intimacy with blacks by appropriating the idiom as though he were one of them. Another *Voice* hand imagines that whites and blacks will shortly be bound so close that familiar color schemes will disappear. "Who's to say that whites who work at it can't be part of a 1990s black 'we'?" this writer asks. "[Phase I] of the American reconstruction project comes in redefining the fictions of blackness and whiteness, and ultimately, in accepting our common Brownness: Black + White + whatever = Brown."

Where blackness and whiteness are conceded to be somewhat more than "fictions," a fix-it mentality enters with preventives and correctives. Academicians outline programs of difference-deleting studies in "interracial competence." Public television produces a news feature—its title echoes Rodney King's words: "Can We All Get Along?"—reporting on successes in interracial collaboration. Minds of every stripe—the professoriat and the upper-middlebrow socially concerned, adpeople and merchandisers, sitcom and film fabricators, politicos and assistant managers—all know that *right feelings* hold the key.

"Racism is silly," says Doug Raboy, adman-head of Citizens for Racial Harmony, a group that installed 250 brotherly love posters in New York City phone booths following the Los Angeles riots. Consensus orthodoxy stakes everything on this binary opposition: friendship versus silliness. A NYNEX public service commercial animates the theme by arraying two sets of multicolored marbles against each other (menacing infantile grunting on the soundtrack); suddenly one marble on each side dares to roll forward toward the other embracingly. Aggies and shooters cheer and mingle like the ballplayers after Billy Hoyle's slam dunk, whereupon camera magic transforms the marbles into the globe.

If you'll just stop being silly, children, if you just for once try being nice *to each other . . .*

Faith in the miracle cure by change of heart is no idiosyncratic hobbyhorse of this or that stage character or novelist or TV pundit. It's the soul of a race discourse of one-on-one that's become so familiar as to be almost unnoticeable, and that has remarkable social range, extending from the PBS essayist's claim that we're all in the same boat to the lovefest of Wal-Mart's Jared and Joseph and Bobbie and Dell.

And the faith is ridden with contradictions. It represents—to repeat—a clear advance from the time when hatred was a norm and educated whites used the abhorrent label "nigger" without qualm. And that time reaches deep into the twentieth century. Long after Reconstruction, mockery and vilification of African Americans were standard in cultural expression extending from defenses of lynching to hostile stereotypes in fiction (Thomas Dixon, Booth Tarkington, and Margaret Mitchell among others) and obnoxious "minstrel" entertainments relished by self-styled respectable citizens. (White man to black woman with a crying child: "Auntie, why's that boy crying? Is he spoiled?" Auntie: "Naw, he ain't spoiled. Dat's his natchal odor.")

It's beyond denial that the end of these barbarities stands as a moral fresh start, regardless of whether professions of white-black friendship are or aren't insincere. It's also plain that works depicting devoted relationships between blacks and whites can exert warmly humanizing influence. They create symbols through which the young and old can grasp the possibility of easy, unforced, mutually enjoyable connection between the races, and they confirm what millions already know: life lived without strong ties to the other race is an impoverishment.

But the new language of concern—the friendship orthodoxy of Bobbie and Dell—*is* multidimensional. A step forward in the nation's moral life, it is also emerging—because of delusions that it inspires—as a political and intellectual step backward. Certainty that one-on-one, black-white personal relations can be relied on to resolve race problems obscures a body of fact—fact about America as an opportunity society attempting to coexist with a castelike society—that's essential to anyone seriously attempting to address issues of race. Consensus thinking leaches away knowledge of the vital connections between the present race situation and the conflicts and injuries from which that situation developed. It lays the groundwork for political attempts to abolish racial categories through law and bureaucratic practice (a "postmodern conspiracy," as one scholar terms it, "to explode racial identity"). Everywhere it discourages effort to conceptualize problems in ways that bring to bear all the truly pertinent knowledge—all that is known about, all that genuinely illuminates, the experience of living African Americans.

It is time now to remind ourselves of the substance of that experience—the texture of the life that vanishes (from majority view but not from minority experience) as accredited delusion takes command.

Chapter 4

Caste Society/
Opportunity Society (I):
An Overview

The shaping influence on African American lives, according to current popular and elite discourse on race, is the goodwill—or the bias and intolerance—of individual white Americans. The far more potent shaping influences are, in reality, history and politics.

Well-intentioned whites grasp that many blacks feel grievances against them. (The grievances are traced to slavery on one hand and to aberrant race hatred on the other.) But well-intentioned whites seldom grasp that attempts to address the grievances through personal gesture (the abolition of bias) cannot reach the broad fundamentals of the African American situation. Owing to a combination of historical and political factors, masses of blacks are caught up in racial stratification; the low-status stamp set on them at birth is, for the majority, not commutable. The various facets of African American human and socioeconomic disaster—joblessness, drugs, crime, family collapse, homelessness, suicide rates—are bound into structural interdependence by the power of this racial stratification; they cannot be coped with as discrete "problem areas." And progress at ameliorating racial stratification is suffering major setbacks now not only because of "conservative backlash" but as the result of broadscale economic trends (deindustrialization, corporate restructuring, the global economy); goodwill cannot alter the effects of these trends.

Stratification is a complex and paradox-ridden subject, to be sure. Black Americans are no longer assigned low status de jure; their position reflects not law but existing social arrangements and individual and family expectations and beliefs. And birth-ascribed status is no longer universal within the black stratum. Census figures show that as many as 8 million African Americans—almost a third of the black population—belong to families with middle-income status: yearly earnings above $35,000. (In 1993 the median U.S. family income—blacks, whites, Hispanics, and all others included—was $37,500.) Many of the country's richest, most admired achievers in sports and entertainment are black, and many black political leaders—Barbara Jordan, Tom Bradley, and Marian Wright Edelman are examples—are accorded affection and respect.

These changes are sometimes spoken of slightingly, as though they were cosmetic—events of little consequence. That position is absurd. No precedent whatever exists for the talent hunts for young black scholars, professionals, and business careerists that are now pressed by educational and corporate institutions at the top of the opportunity society; African Americans perceived as truly promising are exhorted in genuinely good faith to compete for places on the highest rungs.

And it's almost certain that this open competition will continue to be held crucial to national identity. The majority culture is wedded to an egalitarian, individualistic, can-do, making-it mythology that stresses inclusiveness; the American Dream, democratic at its core, is presumed to include everybody. This traditional ideal of openness undergirds faith in the new ways of thinking already sampled in these pages—faith that blacks and whites are the same and that surviving vestiges of hostility stem only from irrational ill will.

For these reasons and others the subject of race stratification, massive in scope, demands nuanced, even delicate treatment. In the American context stratification involves double truth, namely that within our borders an opportunity society and a caste society coexist.

The leader of the effort to explain and document ascribed status in America—the most respected researcher in the field—is the gifted anthropologist John Ogbu of the University of California at Berkeley. Nigerian by birth, Ogbu plainly cares deeply about the situation of American blacks; occasionally his frustration at continuing American obtuseness about stratification crops out in phrases appearing to depreciate the economic gains of the achieving third of the country's black population. But Ogbu's contributions (and those of the school he founded) rank, overall, as extraordinary. Possessing an unmatched comparatist's eye for commonalities in the situations of African Americans and bottom-strata populations elsewhere, he's amassed compelling evidence of the operations of ascribed inferior status as a defining influence in the lives of millions of American blacks. Without his work it would be difficult indeed to keep in clear view the facts of experience that the new friendship jargon obscures—impossible, perhaps, to defend oneself against moral fantasy.

Not long ago the need for a defense was less pressing, partly because the rule against speaking of America as a racially stratified, or castelike, society was less stringent. As recently as the late 1970s, Establishment authority could state, undemonstratively, that despite the accomplishments of the Civil Rights Movement, most black Americans experience castelike status of inferiority. A president of the American Psychological Association—MIT professor Kenneth Keniston—wrote, in

1978, that the country should discard "the ideological blinders by which we rationalize the persistent inequities of our social system, and confront the fact that ours remains in a real sense a caste society." In the same year the Carnegie Foundation's Council on Children—one of the members was Marian Wright Edelman—enthusiastically published Ogbu's own definitive study of likenesses between the situation of blacks in America and that of certain castes abroad—untouchables in India, Buraku outcastes in Japan, Oriental Jews in Israel, Maoris in New Zealand. (Professor Keniston hailed the work on its appearance as belonging to "the same tradition and [deserving of] the same influence as Gunnar Myrdal's *An American Dilemma.*")

But the changes that would in time shunt caste scholarship to the margins were well advanced at that very moment. The country was midway through a period (1970–1990) that would record the fastest ever twenty-year rise in black income. The impact of affirmative action, federal and state provision of "set aside" appropriations for minority contractors, and expanded educational opportunities was being felt in African American communities and beyond. The latest cycle of majority concern with minority hardship—the past century and a half has witnessed several such cycles— had reached and passed its peak. Racism-is-over messages in *The Cosby Show* vein were attracting mass audiences.

And significant shifts of perspective were taking

place in other sectors. Responding to subtle changes in the climate of opinion, and to objectively measurable changes in employment patterns, academic experts on black America were beginning to probe connections between race and the emerging economic structures. William Julius Wilson, for one, made his reputation with a work that studied employment and family structures in the ghetto; the book proclaimed end-of-racism orthodoxy in its title (*The Declining Significance of Race,* 1978) as well as in its text. The so-called underclass, moreover, was becoming a preferred topic for newsmagazines in this period; it was presented as "a state of mind and a way of life," a criminal fringe traceable not to the history of race stratification but either to the advent of widespread immoral behavior or to the combination of unprecedented sociopolitical forces—deindustrialization, urban decay, ill-conceived welfare programs—on which Wilson concentrated. The emerging theme was that race itself had ceased to be the American dilemma, that racism wherever it lingered was "a psychodynamic phenomenon characteristic of [maladjusted] individuals," and that the country's real problems were vice, crime, family disintegration, corporate restructuring and unemployment, the collapse of public education, and the death of cities.

Scholars who continued to focus on race stratification were aware that, in the 1990s, that subject needed to be viewed in the context of the global economy. They knew as well that direct race animus could not be blamed for the intensification of efforts to downplay race as a major influence on the social textures of American life. Those efforts reflected many positive elements—decent hope, longing for relief from race anguish, eagerness for a final end to "the color line." But caste scholars were and remain convinced that turning away from stratification—denying its influence—is an act of unaffordable wishfulness that spawns dangerous moral delusions.

The chief delusion, simply stated, is that the practical human effects of the history of race stratification have somehow been canceled by the signing of legislative and judicial papers "awarding" civil rights, by improvements in the status and earnings of a third of the black population, and by the appearance of a new popular mythology of equality and sameness. Caste scholarship argues that this delusion, a serious barrier to straight thinking about race, weakens the nation's capacity to name its race problem truthfully, much less to engage it.

Taking the measure of the barrier directly, spelling out how and why castelike stratification can exist in a culture of opportunity, means running two risks: that of appearing to speak a forbidden language and that of appearing pedantically to explain the obvious. On the American race front there is no easy escape from the double bind.

Benjamin DeMott

"Prejudice" Versus Stratification

"Race prejudice" is a feeling of hostility within individuals; race stratification, or caste, encompasses race
prejudice but isn't identical to it, and the difference between the two matters intensely even in societies where
there's upward movement within the bottom caste. The
difference holds the key, in fact, to the difficulty of ending racism.

In one dimension race stratification is a principle by
which caste societies and castelike societies in transition
determine, by race, the allocation of desirable and undesirable work. In another dimension race stratification
is a principle determining the organization of education;
tightly connected to the principle relating to allocation
of work, this principle ordains that the large majority of
one race will be educationally prepared for desirable
work, and the large majority of the other for undesirable work. In yet another dimension race stratification
consists not of principles but of stories—explanatory
materials that enable the primary majority and subordi-
nate minority to make sense of (and peace with) the
distribution of jobs, power, and relative good fortune.

These stories are no minor elements in the structure
of caste; they are narrative rationales determining attitudes, expectations, motivations, habits, skills, and values. And, because bottom-caste and mainstream stories
differ vastly from each other, they (in combination with

the differences in work, property, and schooling that they "explain") effectively locate most of the bottom caste and most of the mainstream in separate psychocultural worlds. There are two evident points of connection: both strata embrace folk as well as pseudoscientific explanations. And within each stratum there's feedback between pop and elite explanations, "so that in the course of time the folk theory becomes modified to look more 'scientific,' especially as 'scientific findings' are mass produced and mass consumed."

But few other points of connection exist. Study of the basic stories accepted in six contemporary caste or castelike societies (the United States among them) on three continents reveals in each instance that ruling assumptions of the bottom caste totally contradict those within the mainstream. This is one reason, obviously, for the weakness of new thinking that stresses black-white sameness. Bottom-caste accounts of inequality and minority "failure" attribute both to an unfair stratification system that whites—people of fundamentally bad character—initiated, support, and manage for their own profit. Mainstream accounts, by contrast, attribute the failure to "the personal, familial, cultural, or biological inadequacies of the minority group." (The arrival of friendship orthodoxy introduced, in America, two stories better fitted to educated tastes; one story attributes black failure partly to the absence of white goodwill; the other—more recent—

attributes black failure to excesses of white goodwill and permissiveness.)

Power and place conjoined with a sense of the "inadequacies" of the undergroup lead overgroups to believe that minorities mainly get what they deserve. (The tone in which this belief is expressed ranges from preceptorial to indifferent to friendly-regretful depending on the culture and the temper of the age.) Impotence together with a sense of the fundamental unfairness of the majority lead bottom castes to reject majority maxims, credos, claims to moral distinction. From these sources—conscious or unconscious condescension on one side, suspicion and distrust on the other—major psychological and behavioral differences arise. The differences persist even after a portion of the bottom caste achieves a measure of upward mobility, and the suspicion and distrust worsen among those left behind.

Grasping what's involved in ending racism demands facing up to the layered structure of stratification—dealing unblinkingly with the interdependency of job ceilings, schooling patterns, and explanatory stories that express and mold attitudes and values on both sides. To oversimplify the realities of stratification is to open the door to fictions—as, for example, that the ascent of a fraction of the bottom caste transforms the feelings and attitudes of the rest of that caste.

It's true that tales of relationships like those of Miss Daisy and Hoke or Bobbie and Dell provide models of right relations between the races that didn't exist a generation ago; it's fiction that these models alter the structural realities of racism. It's true that banishing offensive labels ("nigger") and prohibiting designated modes of discrimination in workplaces and elsewhere improves the nation's moral climate; it's fiction that these steps markedly change the distribution of work opportunities for the majority of black Americans—a key structural reality of racism. It's true that majority concern about minority "educational deficits" reflects a degree of humanity and compassion that would have given heart to the white leaders who, like Eleanor Roosevelt, were struggling for the black cause in the 1930s and 1940s—and the same holds for announcements, official and unofficial, that the whole of the nation's citizenry is now in the same boat; it's fiction that this progress sounds the death knell of caste in America.

Castelike societies tend to be fiction prone at the top. Even societies that are professedly determined to dismantle caste usually fail to recognize the complexity of the issues with which they're dealing. Social problems are almost never analyzed in their embeddedness in racial stratification as a system—in a reality involving, that is, both objective conditions of work, schooling, and income, and subjective interpretations of advantage and adversity.

Benjamin DeMott

Frustrations—National and International—of Caste Dismantling

Recent patterns of caste and caste dismantling in foreign societies and in the United States reveal several important common elements. The first is the existence of an out-group consigned for an extended period to bottom-dog work and status, denied education (directly or indirectly), and long held in contempt by the majority.

Examples aside from American blacks are the segregated Buraku outcastes in Japan, called *Eta* (meaning "full of filth"), whose work background lies in the "polluting" occupation of slaughtering and skinning animals; Oriental or African-Asian Jews in Israel, called *shchorim* (meaning "black ones"), performers of "menial tasks" and farm labor; scheduled castes in India, called "untouchables" and also regarded as polluting—sweepers, scavengers, washermen, and laborers; Maoris in New Zealand, described as "dirty, happy-go-lucky, lazy, improvident" folk and diagnosed in works of social science as lacking "achievement motivation" owing to "weak ego" and as suffering from an "imagination deficiency."

A second element common to caste societies in recent times is the onset, among majorities, of embarrassment and/or disturbance at seemingly inhumane treatment of the minority. Moved by a sense of inequity, the majority takes cautious steps to modify discriminatory practices, to lift job ceilings, and to introduce preferential arrangements. The principal focus of these reform efforts is education, on the assumption that the cause of caste inferiority is mental backwardness or educational deficiency. (It's worth noting that new thinking in America softens this account of the causes of caste inferiority by emphasizing white attitudes as partly responsible for black troubles.)

Examples: America institutes Head Start; Britain streams West Indian children in special classes to meet "their educational needs"; Israel introduces second-chance educational programs for Oriental Jews, together with new curricula stressing "cognitive development"; India's government institutes school lunch programs for untouchable children, as well as "protective discrimination" for scholarship and university places, and a quota system to recruit untouchables for government jobs; New Zealand foundations support remedial educational programs and scholarships for Maoris, and the government makes available civil service jobs, "especially in positions which have to do with direct service to the Maori community."

The third common element in contemporary caste and castelike societies is the fairly rapid fading of hope and expectancy among the bottom caste, as it becomes clear that, despite so-called reform, meaningful advance within the lowest stratum will be limited to a minority rather than be available to all. Educational opportunities either fail to materialize for the majority of caste members or fail to improve access to higher-level jobs. Alienation and distrust are intensified by continuing dominant-group confidence in its moral superiority and expressed determination to change bottom-group values.

Examples outside America: Offered "the shadow but not the substance of assimilation," Maoris aren't "provided with any material incentives to overcome their disillusionment or to work as hard as the [Europeans] in school." Worsening dropout rates, anger at chiding about their "undependableness," and other problems testify to caste disillusionment. In London West Indian youngsters withdraw, demoralized, from schoolwork "no matter how we try to advise and help them," employment officers report. Caste members believe job competition is stacked against them.

The fourth common element is the fairly rapid resurfacing—in majority explanations of the failure of first tentative attempts at caste dismantling—of the theme of caste inferiority. Barely acknowledging the problem of traditional job ceilings (and negative attitudes flowing from them), as well as broader problems of minority distrust, dominant groups return to their original position, stressing—often in pseudoscientific studies—bottom-caste inability to "compete as equals" and bottom-caste responsibility for declining educational and work standards.

In India "the increasing participation of the [untouchables] in public school education [is] associated with deterioration in the quality of these schools and the withdrawal of the upper castes into private schools." The assumption is that every untouchable is incompetent; a member of the caste "holding a scholarship or a good job got it because of government preferential treatment and not because of his own ability." (A similar assumption figures in some U.S. talk—audible at its harshest on call-in radio—regarding affirmative action.) In England racial stereotypes reappear in public print—arguments, that is, that Caucasians are "more intelligent than either Negroids or Mongoloids." In Israel "the popular explanation" of Oriental Jews' failures holds that "Orientals are not able to learn the 'higher cultures' and skills taught by the schools because their cultural backwardness and the 'negative' influences of their families and neighborhoods all combine to produce inferior mental capacity."

Resurgent discourse on inferiority is coupled—paradoxically—with public assertions that racism is over. (Indian social scientists assert that "the problem of untouchability" has been solved; both the Japanese government and Japanese social scientists deny "the existence of a Buraku problem"; American friendship orthodoxy asserts the declining significance of race.)

The issues of genetic superiority and inferiority that repeatedly reach boiling point as individual nations launch projects of caste dismantling stand well beyond settlement. John Ogbu's studies of caste societies led him to conclude that "the genetic potential of any group" lodged in such a society "cannot be fully assessed until that group has been given the maximum opportunity to develop such potential," and in no case yet studied "has such an opportunity been given." The only solid piece of evidence scholars possess comes from, as it happens, studies comparing the performance, in America, of immigrants to this country from Japanese Buraku outcastes with the performance, here, of immigrants from Japanese nonoutcastes. "On the whole, the study revealed that compared to the other Japanese immigrants, the Burakumin achieved superior economic status in the United States. In the area of formal education, the study found no difference in achievement between outcaste and non-outcaste Japanese children in American schools."

The reason appears to be that the former filthy people and their children "are no longer overwhelmed by the traditional prejudice and discrimination *associated with caste status per se.*" In their new environment, "they have as much opportunity as the other Japanese immigrants to improve their social and occupational status through individual efforts, whether through formal education or other means."

As this summary suggests, recent patterns of majority-minority caste developments in other countries show certain parallels to patterns familiar in the United States. Dominant groups tend to downplay the effects of historical degradation on outcaste groups. Dominant groups expect swift results from civil rights declarations and other evidences of goodwill. Dominant groups appear convinced that bottom-caste problems of advancement are largely educational and might best be left to the schools. Dominant groups regard their own acknowledgment that they once bore ill will toward bottom castes as the crucial event in the history of those castes. The majorities within the bottom castes, for their part, experience growing frustration and embitterment upon realizing that this acknowledgment, or change of heart, is widely regarded by the overgroups as sufficient in itself to transform bottom-caste lives.

But comparisons on this model, while helpful in their suggestion that American disappointment with caste-dismantling efforts is by no means unique, suffer from abstractness. To come fully to grips with stratification in this country, it's essential to step closer to local particulars.

Chapter 5

Caste Society/
Opportunity Society (II):
Local Facts

Workplace stratification in America was for generations
entirely straightforward. Black jobs included common
and farm labor, personal and domestic service, and, at
the top, semiskilled labor; white jobs were located above
this ceiling and included skilled labor, clerical and sales
work, and professional, technical, managerial, and pro-
prietorial positions. Education and training were
adapted to the distribution of occupations. Not until
well into the 1960s did this country put itself on record
as determined to provide blacks with an education that

would enable them to win job status and social status equal to those of whites.

What the society had in mind until then was that the black labor force should be trained and educated in a manner that would enable it, without altering the established order of primacy and subordination, to assist the dominant majority in meeting changing sociotechnological needs. Initially, in the pastoral economy, sociotechnological change was negligible; blacks as slaves could therefore be excluded from education and training. Under the pressures of industrialization and, later, war, majority purpose was served by opening up "manual" or "industrial" training to blacks and, still later, by providing institutions in which blacks could train for professional careers in law, medicine, and the ministry. (Controls of several types protected established primacy and subordination: school financing arrangements ensuring the low quality of black education, exclusion of blacks from craft unions, laws specifying that black professionals could be employed only by black clients or congregations.)

The stories and other interpretative devices by which whites made sense of these arrangements stressed, at their most general, the superiority of the one race and the inferiority of the other. Owing to social change, shifts of emphasis in the stories occurred fairly frequently. In the periods when blacks were excluded from schooling, white explanations variously reflected belief that schooling would breed discontent, or that it would make blacks less useful as workers, or that blacks could not learn (because of inferior intelligence). A tacit understanding, in the post-Reconstruction decades, was that the new tenant farming system positively required the denial of schooling to blacks: "the tenant system would break down if black children, as future laborers, received the same kind of education as whites, since such education would encourage them to question the high rates of interest and the exploitative methods of account keeping used by the planters."

But no revision of white explanatory narratives ever significantly modified the assumption that the allocation of work and opportunities for development was the result, rather than the cause, of inferiority. Common sense might hold that the denial of schooling and chances to advance beyond donkey jobs would have to be considered causes of the caste's presumed "incapacities" or "inadequacies." But in America as in other castelike societies the dominant majority reckoned otherwise, invariably holding the distribution of work and education to be a function of inferiority, not the other way round. The broad etiological understanding remained fixed: castelike law and custom, including rigid job ceilings for blacks, were dictated by the obvious fact of black inferiority.

The minority told itself a different story: existing conditions result not from black deficiencies but from the harsh unfairness of majority rules and practices. Down through the generations from David Walker's

Appeal (1829), which reviled whites for "keep[ing] us in wretchedness and misery, to enrich you and your children," through Frederick Douglass's "Resolution," which, in 1846, attacked the majority as a "great aggregation of hypocrites, thieves and liars," and Martin Delany's *Condition* (1852), which denounced whites as "heartless men," to the black preachers of Mobile, Alabama, who sermonized on whites in the 1860s as "white devils" and "demons," belief in white meanness and selfishness—total moral turpitude—remained unshaken. And the belief continues to resound in African American political, pseudoscientific, and pop discourse into our own time (Malcolm X almost to the end of his life, Ice Cube, Chuck D, Professor Jeffries), shaping the conviction of millions that the true reason for black suffering lies in the cold unfeelingness of the white heart.

In the 1960s, with a new majority culture sensibility taking form, laws were passed forbidding discrimination on the basis of race and encouraging preferential treatment for qualified blacks. Shortly thereafter the pace of economic progress quickened. Job ceilings were raised. College-educated blacks found work—often in the public sector—in which there was a reasonable relationship between their academic credentials, salary, and duties. The proportion of blacks with middle-income status rose from 15 percent to nearly 30 percent within a generation. And the emergence of a visible black middle class, small but not negligible, inspired the transformation, in the media, of images of black America (the new doctrines of sameness through sympathy were first expressed through these images).

These changes drew the opportunity society into unprecedented adjacency with bottom-caste life. African American achievers—professionals who lived and consumed luxuriously and taught their children to expect much of life—became familiars, through the instrument of sitcoms, of impoverished blacks as well as of well-off whites. Messages of friendship and mutual concern came to permeate American culture at every level. And the combination of economic advance and cultural themes of amity induced many in white America to believe that fixed lines between the races no longer existed anywhere except in the minds of irresponsible agitators adept at fanning old hostilities for personal advantage.

That belief isn't easily substantiated. The economic, political, and cultural changes of the past half century are of large consequence; some developments accompanying them—*black* flight in appreciable numbers to middle-class suburbs, for one example—would have seemed, not long ago, nearly unimaginable. But a quantity of evidence attests that the changes have failed to erase the marks of caste from American society. Among the most telling evidence on this point is that, today, both the majority and the minority explain the status of bottom-caste blacks in terms that differ little from those that each used for the same purpose in the pre–Civil Rights era.

The minority clings, that is, to its judgment of

whites as selfish, morally duplicitous, and coercive—
and for clear reasons. College-educated blacks are better off, but they're considered to have paid for their
advance by undergoing a process of quasi-whitening,
and they're known to constitute only a fraction of the
minority; the employability and mobility of the mass of
working-class blacks—grandchildren of elders shame-
lessly exploited by whites—have not greatly improved.
In some urban areas where black flight has occurred,
black jobless rates among those left behind are six to
seven times higher than the national average. (In South
Central Los Angeles, in 1990, nearly half the young
adult black males had not only been jobless for the past
year but hadn't sought work for at least that long.)
Urban schools attended mainly by blacks are often in
ruins, and social misery is incomparably worse among
bottom-caste blacks than among whites.

Furthermore, references by whites to black "cultural deprivation" or "educational deficits" encode—as
most blacks hear them—white readiness to blame
blacks for behaving in ways that merely represent efforts to adjust to long-standing white rules, practices,
and personal assessments. A common surmise is that
white declarations of equality between the races—white
affirmations of the onset of an age of fraternal feeling—
are continuous with the hypocrisy and duplicity of the
past; whites speak the upbeat language of all-in-the-
same-boatism as a means of shedding their obligations
to act in support of real equality. Like the members of

many another bottom caste, in short, the majority of this country's bottom caste connect their misfortune with the character of the overgroup; they doubt that the behavior whites recommend—namely that blacks should emulate whites—deserves serious regard as a route to salvation.

Not the least significant symptom of this doubt is bottom-caste distrust of white-approved institutions, such as schools. Dr. James Comer of Yale's Department of Clinical Psychiatry reports a representative example of that distrust: "a black first-grade teacher in an inner-city school with a nearly all-black student body recall[s] explaining classroom rules on the first day. When she finished, a six-year-old raised his hand and said, 'Teacher, my mama said I don't have to do anything you say.' "

Among whites, by contrast, doctrines of sameness and equality arising from the euphoric middle 1960s and subsequent black economic progress—friendship orthodoxy, that is—are under mounting pressure from the right. The doctrines are aggressively pushed, as we've seen, and reports of black income gains are seized on eagerly. But yesteryear's public optimism is, even so, clearly waning. Jim Crow has been abolished, preferential recruitment and advancement have been instituted, whites in number extend the hand of fellowship sincerely, efforts are made to introduce the egalitarian, individualistic philosophy of the opportunity culture to the ghetto, hatred and harassment of blacks are seen as the exception not the rule.

Yet rates of progress are slowing. Black crime and dropout rates worsen; child pregnancies increase. Serious, well-financed efforts to find and support promising African American talent seem not to rouse broad-based enthusiasm among the black population. Outbreaks of black hostility—including separatist behavior on college campuses—grow more frequent. Black leaders themselves speak and write of a split within their people, a widening gap between middle-income achievers and the much larger group at the bottom. Some leaders have actually taken to denouncing the latter for laziness, lack of will, "opportunity aversion."

The result among whites has been a surge of complex countercurrents to friendship orthodoxy—the resurfacing, not invariably oblique and tactful, of the old, internationally familiar theme of caste genetic inferiority. In late 1994 a rash of social science treatises centered on performance on IQ tests reported the "discovery" that, probably owing to bad genes, blacks are mentally inferior. The authors and backers of the thesis carefully observed the manners of friendship orthodoxy. Charles Murray, J. Philippe Rushton, and Seymour Itzkoff each wrote without trace of master race jubilation, sounding troubled by the news their "science" obliged them to broadcast; the words "unfortunately" and "disappointingly" recurred often in their discourse, and the notes of condolence and frustration that they struck reaffirmed white sympathy and concern.

But these notes failed to mitigate the caste anger stirred by the reframing—as a "discovery"—of racist views once thought of as beyond rehabilitation. Natural scientists demolished the social scientists' discovery as a hoax, citing—among a score of persuasive points—the complete absence of connection between genes related to skin color and genes related to cognitive ability. But for many months *The Bell Curve* was seriously "debated" by dozens of white "authorities" and remained high among the fastest-selling books in the country— proof, in the eyes of many African Americans, of where the country's true sympathies lie.

Castelike patterns are, in sum, everywhere discernible in contemporary interracial perceptions. Minority frustration at new rationalizations of old broken promises of equality further hardens long-held convictions of the majority's immorality and self-delusion. And these new rationalizations simultaneously encourage positive self-assessment by well-meaning whites. (Should not whites be proud of the patience and tenacity of their democratic embrace of unequal blacks as equals?) Objective inquiry establishes that, for the majority of African Americans, job ceilings outlawed in principle survive in fact and that "equal schooling" and equal opportunity haven't been attained; black and white explanations of these conditions are diametrically op-

posed; each side's commitment to its favored explanation is strengthened, not weakened, by personalizing
dogmas of sympathy and one-on-one goodwill. In the
mid-1990s these are among the essentials of America's
continuing castelike stratification.

Beneath these essentials, here as in other castelike societies, lie weighty truths of damage and injury. Whites
who acknowledge the truths—who concede the existence of African American injury stemming from the
past—risk being held responsible for the injury. Blacks
who admit that past injuries haunt the present risk lowering their defenses against the charge of "inferiority."
But these evasions are unaffordable: straight thinking
about race stratification depends on a fair accounting of
damage and injury.

Caste scholarship often begins its survey of injury by
focusing on the inferior education provided to blacks
and its cumulative effects over generations. But schooling and the closely related job ceilings and indoctrination in low self-esteem are only parts of the
configuration set under study. More important are the
divergent beliefs and behavior prevailing in the two,
relatively separate, psychocultural worlds—especially
the beliefs and behavior that are pertinent to aspirations
to self-betterment.

On this front damage and injury manifest themselves in bottom-caste black disbelief in the world as

pliant to the individual will and in bottom-caste skepticism about qualities regarded as indispensable in ambitious people hoping to bend experience to their desire. John Ogbu notes that white status mobility systems envisage a mechanistic world that can be moved by the lever of personal intention; they "encourage the development of such personal qualities as independence, foresight, initiative, industriousness, and individualistic competitiveness"—qualities seen as supportive of the quest for self-improvement and control over external situations.

For most blacks experience still points in a different direction, advising against belief that individuals can exercise shaping power over external situations. Generations have learned, in anger or otherwise, that "reliance on white patronage [is] the most effective approach to self-betterment" and that the truly vital personal qualities are "dependency, compliance, and [adeptness at] manipulation." Ogbu cites a colleague's conclusion: "Neither Uncle Tom . . . nor the black militant ever gains control over the situation at hand; [instead], they *manipulate* whites whom they confront to avoid thrashing, to gain a gratuity, or to gain public exposure which might result in a token reward."

Bitterness attends this learning, assuredly. But the majority of African Americans nevertheless do not hunger to trade the substance of experiential lessons for the white belief system. In waging their "collective struggle to achieve equality with whites," Ogbu writes, they necessarily sharpened a sense of separateness, "forging a collective social identity that is oppositional or ambivalent toward the white American identity." Over the years they've taught themselves to reject "specific behaviors, events, symbols . . . as not appropriate for themselves because they are characteristic of white Americans." (A black parent who encourages her first-grader to resist and disobey a black teacher in a black school is committing such an act of rejection.) Often their way of defining what's "appropriate or even legitimate for themselves" has been through direct contrast with positions approved by the majority—through "opposition to the attitudes . . . of white Americans, who are their 'enemies' or 'oppressors.' " A not insignificant concept of treachery among blacks has its origin in scorn of members of the race "who try to behave like whites (i.e., to 'cross cultural boundaries' into forbidden domains)," whether in schools or elsewhere.

When the scorn surfaces in children, says Yale's James Comer, parents often don't contend against it because of their own consciousness of "animosity and rejection by the mainstream." Comer emphasizes the element of self-protectiveness in black children's mockery of "good"—i.e., white-imitating—black pupils. Seeing "academic success as unattainable," he argues, these children "protect themselves by deciding school is unimportant. [They] seek a sense of adequacy, belonging and self-affirmation in nonmainstream groups that do not value academic achievement."

Discussing "the deep distrust [blacks] have developed for white Americans and for the institutions, such as the public schools, controlled by white people," Ogbu himself speculates that its roots lie in early demands that, in exchange for acceptance, blacks "must abandon their own cultural norms . . . and embrace those of the white community." This forced "rehabilitation process" (common in other castelike societies), together with its failure to bring the promised acceptance, caused blacks to "invest positive values in the very cultural norms [and] behaviors . . . denigrated by white people."

But whatever the precise processes of its engendering, and despite the widespread delusion that rights laws, goodwill, and a measure of economic progress for a third of the population must by now have banished it, the distrust still runs deep. Nor, contrary to yet another national myth, does the distrust have any real counterpart in the sensibility of the voluntary immigrant minorities with whom blacks are regularly compared. Again the authoritative comment is that of John Ogbu: "Unlike the caste groups," he writes, "immigrant minorities operate outside the beliefs of an established system of social hierarchy and are not deeply affected by the ideology of superiority and inferiority that supports such a hierarchy." The voluntary minorities were never prompted to rage by "the loss of their freedom, their displacement from power, and the deprivation of property"; they do not see "present barriers against them as institutionalized"; their experience doesn't teach them that "future improvements [demand] a collective struggle against their 'white oppressors.' " They came to the United States "voluntarily because they believed that immigration would lead to more economic well-being, better overall opportunities, or greater political freedom. These expectations continue to influence the way in which [they] perceive and respond to their treatment by white Americans."

Much of the injury to African Americans caused by educational deprivation, demeaning job ceilings, and ascribed inferiority can be read in the look of urban places, in street drunkenness, gang gunfire in projects, whole schools engaged in teaching child-mothers how to discharge parental responsibilities. But a fair accounting reaches beyond the visible into the interaction of majority and minority minds and feelings. Caste injury is reflected in the assumptions common among teachers black and white as they confront black pupils, namely that most of the latter face by necessity a limited future (job ceilings masked but still in place), that they will not or cannot excel at schoolwork, that special efforts to help them are likely to be unavailing, that burdening them with expectations is the opposite of kindness, and that none of the foregoing assumptions should be thought of as causing the pupils' academic performance.

Caste injury is equally reflected in most black pupils' preparation for and adaptation to these unvoiced messages: preparation that reveals itself in guardedness, quickness to sense humiliation, anticipation of defeat, angry (and parentally supported) rejection of claims that failure is in any measure the pupil's "own fault." And caste injury is reflected in the atmosphere of predetermination existing not only in classrooms wherein these assumptions lock on to one another but in the larger society as well.

This is only to repeat that race stratification isn't a mere matter of degree of access to good schools, jobs, and housing. It includes the treatment of most members of the minority not in sitcoms and ads but in the real world and the responses of the minority to that treatment. Rap lyrics expressing violent detestation of whites, poll results showing that few African Americans believed O. J. Simpson could receive a fair trial, a black prosecutor's absolute certainty, at Simpson's trial, that the revelation of a city detective's use of the word "nigger" would guarantee an innocent verdict from the largely black jury—these responses occasion shock or mystification. But in truth they, like most black responses, are only partly understood when judged in accordance with the majority frame of reference. African American resistance bespeaks, undeniably, injury suffered in the past, and more than a few white observers have held that the resistance is incapacitating. But the mass of resisters, silent or militant, see their resistance in other terms—as a distrust profoundly grounded in moral reason. And they, too, are correct; their understanding, a major element of the content of caste, and rarely if ever fully comprehended by whites, has dignity of its own.

Chapter 6

Caste Society/
Opportunity Society (III):
The Problem of
Change Rates

Caste scholarship is especially penetrating on the subject of change and progress. It throws clear light on feasible rates of progress. It provides warnings about hidden obstacles. It helps to explain why certain well-intended white gestures and policies tend to slow the very advance they're meant to speed. Some policies fail either because they rush to evaluation too swiftly or—contrariwise—because they take the avoidance of evaluation to be an act of beneficence. Others fail because they're heedless of African American resentment of blacks selected for special privilege by white masters—

resentment stretching deep into the slave past. The key mistake to which caste scholarship draws attention is that of assuming middle-income status to be the norm in black America.

Item: Intent on showing generalized goodwill, teachers of black pupils shut their eyes to the kinds of educational labor necessitated by caste stratification. In one American city 94 percent of minority students over a period of four years received the same grade: C. Grade awards acknowledging improved levels of application were nonexistent, and written assessments and letter grades nowhere matched; "a child who receive[s] a C rating in grade one continues to receive the same rating in subsequent years, although the teacher at each grade level writes that she is 'delighted' at his 'progress.'" The link between hard work and reward—the labor → achievement equation—is a commonplace in the middle class; failure to teach it in the bottom castes, a much larger cohort, is the opposite of kindness; it's an obstacle to future learning.

Item: Affirmative action programs customarily bestow advantage on beneficiaries already possessing middle-income status—people regarded warily by the majority of the black population as sellouts who made their way by "acting white." (Most African American students admitted to elite educational institutions, for example, are the children of generations of perceived black privilege.) Even a token program to facilitate the mobility of black working-class youth would be of use, but none flourishes. The situation is exacerbated by the rise of middle-class blacks to administrative posts in welfare and related programs, with affirmative action assistance; from these heights the appointees condescend to their minority clients, even using the phrase "the underclass" when speaking of them. The effect is to intensify negative feelings about ambition, mobility, "success."

Item: Ignoring the cumulative impact of generations of race stratification, educational authority habitually exaggerates the pace at which compensatory educational programs can produce measurable results. The programs aim at changing attitudes and behavioral patterns that were formed over centuries. But, driven by a continuity-erasing evaluation anxiety that all castelike societies seem to share, authorities wait only weeks or months before deploying tests—as though desperate for scientific proof that the majority's belated commitment to interracial equality is justifiable on rational grounds.

Because the history of America as a castelike society is seldom in view, the culture remains convinced that racism is an affliction of individual neurotic whites. And that conviction blinds officials and laypersons alike to essential truths about the nature of the transition from behaviors befitting a society of caste barriers to behaviors befitting a society attempting, erratically, to dismantle caste barriers. Exaggeration is the rule in accounts of the socioeconomic progress of the black population as a whole. Misconceptions about *possible* rates of economic and educational progress are rife. Attentiveness to complications arising from black oppositional will and distrust is rare.

These points are repeatedly stressed in public comments by professionals now laboring creatively in America's caste-dismantling effort. The nation's most widely admired, innovative ventures in minority education are the several dozen "social development" public schools, which, in communities from New Haven, Connecticut, to Lee County, Arkansas, are building groups of teachers, parents, job trainers, employers, and community leaders—collaborators seeking to cope simultaneously with problems ranging from job ceilings to parental alienation. The key figure in the creation of these schools, James S. Comer, loses no opportunity to set basic problems of trust—and facts about the probable pace of progress—before the general public.

Comer notes that bottom-caste parents lose hope and confidence fast, become defensive and hostile, avoid contact with school staffs. And he insists that the time frames to which conventional social science is habituated are irrelevant to the ventures on which development schools are launched. His views on the subject were well summarized in a recent *New Yorker* article on his work by William Finnegan:

"On the average, [Comer] estimates, three generations of continuous access [to the development school experience] are necessary if a family is to gain the type of education that will allow its members to function successfully in the postindustrial economy. But few black families had achieved that continuity before deindustrialization began to shatter the hopes of working-class people. 'Large and pervasive as the drug problem is, it's still only a symptom,' Comer says. 'It's like the headache one gets with a cerebral hemorrhage. It's not the headache that's going to kill you; it's the hemorrhage.' And the hemorrhage in this case, he says, is the profound, ongoing failure to educate poor [black] Americans."

A culture conversant with the nature of race stratification here and abroad would acknowledge that failures to undo caste often result from fantasy-inspired time frames for "progress," and that, for two thirds of the African American population, the work of undoing centuries of caste has barely begun.

It would acknowledge, further, that if a castelike society funds two dozen or so social development schools for a maximum of ten years when the need is for several hundred such schools in full operation over longer than a half century, the society should expect to wait for more than two to three generations for the transition from caste to noncaste behavior to complete itself. It would acknowledge that the cause of minority-majority trust can be forwarded only marginally by policies that distribute mobility advantages to a small percentage of a race cohort while denying advantages to the rest. And it would acknowledge that explanations of race violence that see it as a response to separate, unassociated provocations—police brutality or joblessness or another discrete cause—oversimplify both the problems and the ameliorative approaches that have a chance of succeeding.

Taking caste reality seriously would mean making *all* these acknowledgments—breaking with friendship orthodoxy, awakening from the trance world wherein rich white lawyers are indistinguishable from impoverished black physical therapists and wherein discount department stores create interracial utopias on their own. It would mean absorbing and acting upon the complex truth of race stratification—confronting the reality of variegation in the black population, recognizing black America as a race cohort including within its ranks many professionals and 2 to 3 million families of middle-income status, yet dominated numerically and psychosocially by an oppressed caste. But it is precisely this reality from which the new thinking—friendship orthodoxy—averts its eyes.

Chapter 7

Invisible Woman:
Friendship Dogma and
the Disappearance of
Joyce Ann Moore

Annually, in criminal and other cases, every urban courtroom hears hundreds of narratives that touch nervously on bottom-caste existence. Summarizing who did what to whom, witnesses are permitted to cast brief, hazy light on the lives of adults who didn't launch on career planning as children because What-do-you-want-to-be-when-you-grow-up? was in their caste a question not asked, who had no reason in youth or later to regard gainful employment within the law as part of the natural order, who were never candidates for initiation into the positive mainstream sense of home, family, school, and work. What's striking in the small dramas played out as these cases are heard is the variety of stratagems employed to assimilate bottom-caste background and history to mainstream middle-class norms.

Ironies multiply quarter hour by quarter hour during examination and argument. When white court-appointed defense attorneys mention mitigating details of a black client's destitution and misfortune, they're often denounced as racist, not uncommonly by black prosecutors. Black prosecutors, middle-income professionals well aware of the caste restrictions on choice that control life at the bottom for most of their race, nevertheless damn the crimes of welfare mothers and pubescent murderers with panegyrics on free will. In closing statements, instructions from the bench, and verdicts, the mantras of new thinking—*The races are equal, the races are the same*—are endlessly repeated. Society acts out, through the justice system, its will to deny its own stratification.

This legal insistence on racial sameness isn't without elevated purpose. By disallowing extended reference to the backgrounds of bottom-caste black defendants, courts mean to deter cynical exploitation of alibis of disadvantage, to erect a barrier against separate and unequal standards of justice, and to preserve the purity of the law's universals ("intent," "individual responsibility," and "free choice").

Closely observed, though, the embrace of sameness and equality dogma in any individual court proceeding usually can be seen to serve other purposes and interests as well—the same interests that rule outside the judicial realm. Whites everywhere seek assurance that they aren't responsible for the misery of great-grandchildren of white-owned slaves. Well-off blacks—legatees of small but not inconsequential advantage within the race over the generations—seek assurance that the sole reason they are placed differently than their bottom-caste black contemporaries is that the latter are irredeemably lazy and slobbish. Society as a whole seeks assurance that its commitments to idealism and discipline remain uncompromised. Court endorsement of concepts of black-white sameness and equality supplies these assurances.

But the judicial denial of truths of caste is significant and revelatory not because it reflects general public opinion and interests. The denial matters for two reasons: first, because it functions as a key tool by means of which the new thinking redefines standards of decency and uprightness; second, because these redefinitions are in the process of stripping educated blacks and well-meaning whites alike of their capacity to contribute to African American advancement.

An example: In 1990 Joyce Ann Moore was a twenty-five-year old African American welfare mother living with her seven children and a boyfriend in Milwaukee's black district. One night while she and the boyfriend were away from home, six of her children burned to death inside. She was charged with six counts of homicidal neglect and one count of simple neglect (the latter pertained to her oldest child, who jumped to safety from a second-story window).

The trial lasted four days. The black prosecutor held that the accused's children died as "the result of [her] intentional acts . . . her intentional failure to supply a baby-sitter. She knew the children were alone." The white defense attorney countered that the mother had in fact made arrangements for baby-sitters before leaving her house, hence couldn't have meant to cause her children's deaths. Out-of-state social workers testified that Joyce Moore had left her children alone before and had been warned against doing so again. Two children (Moore's thirteen-year-old nephew and the daughter who survived the fire) and three adults (Moore's two sisters and an elderly male neighbor) testified that on neither this occasion nor any other had Moore left her children unattended.

Agreeing with the prosecution, the jury (ten whites, two blacks) found the defendant guilty; the sentence was seven years of jail time.

The details of the defendant's life story composed a familiar bottom-caste narrative. Joyce Moore drops out of school, in Dyersburg, Tennessee, in the early 1980s. She is fourteen years old, pregnant, and barely literate; she has no family support system, and the town offers no counseling, "further educational opportunity," or publicly financed child care. Each of the three men by whom she bears children in the next few years deserts her.

Comment on Moore in social service files reveals familiar patterns of disorder and incapacity. Observing young children playing naked in the dirt in front of a dilapidated house, a passerby phones the town office. A social worker visits and finds no grown-up home. An infant sits on the stove next to a lighted gas burner. Another child, seated on the feces-strewn kitchen floor, is trying to open a can of food with a meat cleaver. Joyce Moore returns shortly; she's been grocery shopping. The social worker tells her she can't leave her children unattended, and Moore answers that a neighbor was checking on them.

A year or so later a police cruiser investigates a complaint about a black female making a public nuisance of herself on a street corner, apparently in the company of several children. The plump-cheeked, physically small eighteen-year-old is begging for money. She's been evicted from a motel where welfare temporarily billeted her and is penniless. The children are teary and hungry. The mother needs a roof, somebody to watch her kids for an hour, money for food, a ride to a 7-Eleven.

Moore moves frequently from dwelling to dwelling, state to state, Tennessee to Illinois, Illinois to Wisconsin. The cycle of loss, defeats large and small, remains the same. The older children flounder in school, and the mother can't help—reading and numbers are beyond her. A social worker describes her as suicidal. The eventual live-in boyfriend—a man named Tommy Smith with a van and a job—consents to work with the kids on their lessons ("Joyce asked me," Smith testifies, "because I might could do better than her"). But Smith suffers a disabling workplace injury.

There are nine human beings—infants, toddlers, a preteen and two adults—and endless scrambling for survival. The round of errands that takes the mother from her children on the evening of the fire is a short catalog of caste mishaps. Moore and Smith pick up a used stove to replace the collapsed stove in Moore's kitchen (they carry the "new" stove down a flight of stairs to Smith's van). They travel to a hospital emergency room hunting a physician's excuse Smith thinks may help him recover his job. At a grocery they buy hot dogs for the children's evening meal and return to drop them off. They visit another store and three apartments looking for Smith's sister (he owes her some money). Moore and Smith have a protracted argument in the van, subject unspecified. During the five-hour peregrination they drink between twenty and sixty ounces of beer (Smith's estimate).

Money trouble, distraction, difficulty clinging to the thread of purpose—bottom-caste norms. Black America includes millions of welfare mothers, the majority overwhelmed by their own lives. Government checks don't cover essentials. (At age twenty, in Decatur, Illinois, Moore had $302 a month on which to support herself and four children.) The mothers are often physically abused. (One of the mates who deserted Moore regularly beat her.) Like Moore, many experience intermittent homelessness. (One landlord locked Moore out and then refused to permit her access to her belongings.) Like Moore, some find uninvited officials in their dwellings—people who deliver threats ("Your children will have to be taken away"). Like Moore, many watch their children duplicate their own school failures and humiliations. When tragedy strikes—the loss of six children they've managed to keep alive through years of privation—some are punished as child killers. (The state jailed Moore on $300,000 bond, denied her the right to talk to her surviving child, and sought to punish her with a sentence of sixty years.)

We do not overgeneralize, in sum, in describing welfare mothers as continuously acted upon, done unto. Need, ignorance, abuse, frustration, confusion, and dislocation are the primary forces visible in their lives; often by early adolescence their self-sovereignty has been irreparably damaged. When the courtroom stilled, Joyce Moore's sobbing was sometimes audible; it wasn't the sound of a person of full agency.

But her case, like numberless parallel cases, is instructive not because of her obvious helplessness but because of counsels' insistence on her capability. Judicial denials of caste truth invariably begin with tacit agreement, by the prosecution and defense, that bottom-caste defendants should be presented as free agents acting and executing on their own, responsible for their choices. In *Wisconsin v. Moore*, that agreement was maintained—with but one momentary and instructive interruption—to the end.

The prosecution represented Moore as a person of criminally neglectful nature who freely and habitually chose evil. Why was a child aged one year found seated by a lighted burner on a stove in a house empty of grown-ups? On the night of the fire, why was no grown-up present in the defendant's house, watchful of her brood of seven, prepared to save them? Because this mother meant her children harm. The district attorney drew forth lengthy testimony on the torture endured by the children caught in the blaze, emphasizing that grotesque thoughts and feelings—Joyce Moore's shutting off her mother love—lead to grotesque ends. (Intense heat caused "skin slippage," "loosening skin from the dermis," turning dark skins pink and filling lungs and stomachs with black soot; carrying the steaming bodies from the house, said a fireman, "was like holding a casserole dish from the oven when you're wearing an oven mitt.")

The defense's Joyce Moore was equally freestanding—not a creature of evil will but quite as detached from the influence of circumstance, race, income. Moore was a capable, caring mother, according to her lawyer. She was aware of the rules that oblige parents to behave forehandedly—to retain sitters, provide them with information regarding emergency help, set rates of pay, and so on. Moore had arranged for her twelve-year-old nephew to look after the seven children on his return from school. She had asked her sisters—near neighbors—to look in at the house while she was gone, and they had. During her errands, she had telephoned another neighbor asking him to check on the children, and he had.

Happenstance was therefore the villain, said the defense. We can't know how fate intervened, how the tragedy occurred—the cause of the fire, the reasons this competent mother's efforts to guard her children's safety ultimately failed. But we do know that the defendant went to lengths to see to it that other caregivers fulfilled the responsibility with which she entrusted them, hence she couldn't be guilty of intentionally harming her own young.

The lawyerly wrangling—the power of evil versus the power of accident—often turned furious. Time and again snippets of "accidental" testimony or courtroom eruptions opened a new window on bottom-caste chaos. Moore's surviving child and a nephew testified that Moore asked them to baby-sit before leaving home. The prosecution called police officers who testified that, at the scene of the fire, both children denied they were baby-sitting. The proceedings were abruptly stopped when a sister of the accused was detected signaling from the spectators' benches to a defense witness—coaching the surviving daughter in midtestimony. Outraged, the judge banished the woman from the courtroom.

Unrelentingly the prosecution hammered at the point that the concern of those described as watching the children was perfunctory if it existed at all. Steadily, as the trial proceeded, a sense of unreality deepened. Reason had to doubt the presence of murderous *intent* in an evicted, penniless mother who begged on street corners for food and shelter for her children, tried unavailingly to help them with schoolwork, and (by supported testimony) called on her sisters and a neighbor to look in on them across the alley when she was gone.

But reason also had to doubt that careless, loosely managed "checking" could be likened, as the defense implicitly likened it, to arrangements conventional in suburban worlds, where sprinklers glint on combed lawns and time is "organized" and nutrition is effortfully balanced and appointment- and lesson-ridden children commence in toddlerdom educations in executive assumption.

Between the pattern of the defendant's life activities—typical bottom-caste activities—and the patterns of orderly existence in suburban Milwaukee or wherever, there was no synchrony; her lawyer was stretching in promoting Moore to the classes that visit "family doctors," replace worn appliances with new ones, and thumbtack prized baby-sitter phone lists to their kitchen bulletin boards. But the prosecutor, in imagining for Moore a purposively malevolent individual will, was stretching equally far. "The problem isn't neglect," said a plausible report by an investigating officer called to the scene where Joyce Moore was begging. "The problem is poverty."

Long ago social science research established that, for bottom-caste mothers, meeting the challenges of child care—providing food, for instance—is often infeasible without action that appears on its face neglectful. It follows from this not that, in deference to the exigencies of poverty, the line between lawful and unlawful behavior should be erased but that, in cases where intent is crucial, notice should be paid to caste influences on individual capacity for purposive action. "Accountability" and "free choice" need to be drawn down from the world of law logic and artificial reasoning into the world of concrete persons—considered realistically in the context of race stratification.

But in the case at hand, as in most comparable cases, no drawing down occurred; the dogmas of sameness and equality forbade explication of differences between mainstream and bottom-caste "caring." The relevant issues—the unavoidable variations, by caste and class, in standards of protectiveness—went unmentioned almost to the end.

*　*　*

Almost to the end. Wisconsin law allows the prosecution both a closing statement and a rebuttal (the defense makes do with a closing statement alone). In his first closing statement, the district attorney mentioned that the accused had no telephone. This, he argued, was further reason that she should have understood (assuming her motives had been good) the indispensability of an on-the-scene baby-sitter; she had no means of putting herself in touch with the children when she was away.

Earlier in the trial, as part of the conventional legal denial of significant difference, the defense attorney had stressed that the jury had a sacred obligation to ensure that the defendant received the same treatment that would be accorded a "wealthy businesswoman from River Hills." ("The symbols of our justice system are the scales equally balanced and the woman with the sword who is blindfolded.") In his closing statement he suggested—suddenly, surprisingly—that the district attorney's telephone comment amounted to moral censure of poverty. "The D.A.," he told the jury, "tells you that this very poor, uneducated black woman in the inner city didn't have a telephone. And so not having a telephone, a poor black woman not having a telephone, is proof of neglect?"

Until this moment, defense and prosecution had scrupulously observed the dictates of friendship orthodoxy, avoiding allusion to color and social condition (except to dismiss them as irrelevant). But here for a second the defense lawyer strayed; for the length of a phrase or two he seemed to be allowing an impulse of fellow feeling to capsize him. Instead of deleting reference to deficiency or weakness wholly from his mind, guarding himself as a person of majority color from any expression of compassion for the situation of the bereaved mother (a situation owing nearly everything to her caste), he spoke as from above to below, and let an accent of pity escape his lips. Having done this, moreover, he went on to worsen matters, by remarking to the jury that "you or I might have not chosen Billy [the nephew] to be our baby-sitter."

A definitive moment—and a disaster for the defense. The words and tone of "very poor, uneducated black woman" broached the sacral understanding, contradicted a law (there is no difference, we are one and the same) higher than that outlawing child neglect.

In fierce response the prosecutor denied he had equated lack of a phone with neglect. "What I said," he explained icily, "was that if she knew she didn't have a phone, [and] she had seven kids in the house, that was a reason for her to be responsible and to have a responsible person there. [Her] not doing that and knowing those things . . . made it a neglectful situation."

But the full power of his rhetorical, fist-thrusting scorn was reserved for the defense as a proponent of double standards.

"One of the things Mr. Plantinga [the defense attorney] said that I couldn't understand," he began softly, "sounded to me like he was speaking out of both sides of his mouth, was with respect to the standards for Joyce Moore. The standards for judging her conduct.

"He said she's a poor, uneducated black woman who doesn't have a phone. . . . And he said, Are we going to hold her to the same standard as we would a white woman who's a businessperson from River Hills?

"I submit to you," said the district attorney, his high-pitched voice rising a little, "I submit to you that that is what we *do*. But it seems to me that Mr. Plantinga said, No, we will hold Joyce Moore to a lower standard, because of her race, because of her income, because of her position.

"And I submit to you that that is patronizing, that it is condescending, that it is paternalistic. To say that because of her race, because of her income, she cannot care for her children— What kind of sense does that make!"

The prosecutor paused only a moment before ending where he began: with a stern claim that the defense was having it both ways, patronizing black folk while claiming that in this chamber and country blacks and whites are equal.

"We know people who are wealthy but are totally irresponsible. We know people that are very poor that are very responsible, both with their children and their affairs. On one hand, Mr. Plantinga says the standards should be the same for everybody who walks into this courtroom. But on the other hand he says we should judge *her* differently."

One could imagine a different sequel for this trial. Guided by his own impulse of pity, the defense attorney might have ventured to argue that the behavior indicted as murderously cruel wasn't the result simply of choices freely and independently made by the accused—might have proposed that, in assessing her nature, the idea of the autonomous self was less helpful than the idea of social character. With the latter idea came the obligation to think simultaneously about Moore's responsibility for the tragedy and about society's responsibility for Moore's situation as a mother.

Predictably the defense didn't move in these directions, didn't break out of the lockstep of friendship orthodoxy. Its "mistake"—however instructive as regards the dynamics of friendship orthodoxy—became simply an opportunity for a restatement of the commonplaces of new thinking: pity is prejudice, pity is condescending, pity is racist. The district attorney seized on the opportunity, riveting attention on the gesture of pity as upon an uncovered cobra, showing jury members how the defendant could be made to disappear: how, that is, a guilty vote could convict not a helpless black woman but the ascendant ghost of Jim Crow. Understanding, perhaps, that its first duty was to reaffirm universal equality, the jury returned a guilty verdict.

* * *

In a society conversant with caste history, this welfare mother's humanity might not have disappeared. Jury members would have known that "low standards of protectiveness" don't invariably represent acts of personal choice. They would have reckoned with contingency—with the truth that lifetimes of hazard and defeat sap the sense of personal potency. (How can the ceaselessly battered see themselves as invincible guardians of their young?) The jury members would have recognized that drawing sharp lines between safety and danger is infeasible in lives wherein risk and dailiness are indistinguishable.

But in contemporary society friendship orthodoxy is draining meaning from the details of "adverse background"—closing the public eye to the substance of bottom-caste difference. Juries themselves become incapacitated—can't decide justly about whether to criminalize a defendant's behavior, won't allow themselves, when weighing a defendant's behavior, to balance her responsibility with society's.

And those best placed to battle the fantasies of black-white sameness lose their taste for combat. Hope for change in the lives of the bottom caste depends on two groups: educated, achieving blacks who are in a position to speak authoritatively about the human reality they've left behind and liberal, well-intentioned whites not yet oblivious of suffering. Each knows the cruelty of the pretense that we are all in the same boat.

But, as the perfectly representative trial of Joyce Ann Moore demonstrates, assent to friendship dogma disables potential leaders of both kinds. In wasteful service of the mystique of equal treatment, the educated black and well-meaning white who fought each other in *Wisconsin v. Moore* gave their whole beings, in the end, to denying that a bottom caste exists. They offered no resistance to the new thinking which is now transforming impulses of fellow feeling into proof of turpitude.

That transformation is, speakingly restrainedly, ruinous for the human essence. If it's true that advantaged whites can't identify with a bottom-caste black—can't utter the words "very poor, uneducated black"—without looking down, it's also true that, without that act of identification, advantaged whites cannot make the cause of racial justice their own. The dogma of race equality as an already achieved condition carries with it—not alone in sitcoms, commercials, and highbrow essays but in real courtrooms and general life as it is—a near injunction against compassion. Current visions of sameness call for acceptance of the notion that, far from being the seed of ultimate interracial solidarity, a clearheaded, feelingful response to inequality is an act of contempt—arrogant and destructive, mean. In this proscription of pity lies the deepest trouble with friendship, and there is only one remedy: recovery of the intellectual and moral realism that dares to face up squarely to the actual consequences of caste.

Chapter 8

Chicken George & Co. Versus History

The most powerful recent examples of moral realism regarding race were those set by Movement leaders during the Civil Rights struggle. They spoke candidly and often about the injury done to their people over the generations. And that theme led them to reflect, unhesitatingly although with pain, on the cultural morass that quasi-empowerment for African Americans would render inevitable.

The subject arose memorably in the keynote address at the Student Nonviolent Coordinating Committee's fourth general conference in Atlanta in 1961. Detailing various meanings of the black campaign for the vote, the speaker—Bob Moses, a Movement hero—bid rights workers acknowledge to themselves and others that they were "asking all white people in the Delta to do something which [isn't asked] of any white people any place." They were asking whites not only to allow "educationally inferior" Negroes to vote but to "elect leaders to preside over what we could call a numerically inferior but educationally superior white elite."

It was apparent to everyone, Moses argued, that this would have to be "push[ed] down the throats of white people in the Delta . . . because they are determined not to have it done." But it should have been no less apparent—to those doing the pushing—that the white resistance, whatever its moral debility, was completely understandable.

The speaker's realism about black-white difference, born in the frustrations of attempting to awaken an appetite for rights in a long-depressed population, didn't induce quietism or sentimental fantasy of the kind that blurs black-white conflict. Moses was unafraid that frank words from him about "inferiority" would somehow add weight to the racist view that equality was unthinkable. The reason was that, like most Movement leaders, Moses knew his history, possessed a clear grasp of the etiology of the educational deficits in question, knew when, how, and why the black bottom caste was made.

For the development and toughening of moral realism, no resource can begin to match the value of historical knowledge. And in the collapse of American moral realism regarding race, no factor has been more crucial than the assault on historical knowledge conducted by this country's mass media.

We shall come to that assault shortly. Just now, though, it's worth pausing to review once more the broad outline of the making of our bottom caste. From the vantage of history, black inferiority is easily recognizable as the result of deliberated policies aimed at curbing the human development of an entire population—policies that determined the character of the American race situation. The constant that has remained fixed from the earliest slave-catching raids in Africa to the latest denials of means of self-improvement is the certainty, shared by the powerful, that a powerless, uneducated, unaspiring black population spells long-term profit for the advantaged. The inception of slave trading coincided with voyages and discoveries that turned European eyes toward new lands offering rich possibilities for exploitation. Technological and commercial change later to be termed the Industrial Revolution was transforming markets, appetites, and manufacturing and distribution systems. Existing capital deployed in traditional ways could not produce a labor supply commensurate with the unprecedented challenges and opportunities. Rationality sought new solutions and at length resolved in favor of procuring free labor by impressing defenseless peoples.

The same rationality dictated the denial of education and other means of Western-style self-development
to these defenseless peoples—African Americans—once
they were here. (The first prohibitions, on punishment
of death, against teaching blacks to read and write were
instituted because of fear of the political consequences
of literacy.) And rationality further dictated the place-
ment of African American workers below the bottom of
society as conventionally understood. In a culture rife
with egalitarian spirit, the possibility existed that whites
and blacks at the bottom might band together against
entrenched privilege; the legal and social positioning of
blacks outside society, as a group without rights, means,
or hope of advancement—nonpeople to be scorned even
by the poor white labor force, however miserable their
lot—markedly decreased the possibility that common
cause could be made.

Patterns of race feeling within every culture are intricate, needless to say. Recent American scholarship is
skeptical of the notion that the intensity of white working-class hostility to blacks was the result solely of
manipulative coaching by the wealthy and privileged.
The hostility arose at least partly, according to David
Roediger, because, from the country's earliest days, "a
large body of [precariously free] whites could imagine
themselves as slaves—and on socioeconomic, as well as
political grounds." Blacks were despised, in other
words, more because they called up in white workers an
actively feared fate than because white workers pas-

sively accepted indoctrination on the great good luck of their whiteness.

Other scholars emphasize—as a further complicating factor—that a brutalized population will inevitably include some who come to behave like brutes; such behavior inspires genuine revulsion, and this in turn makes it easier for the brutalizers to see themselves as policers, not causers, of brutishness.

But if it's clear that the patterns of exploitation of African Americans are at every historical moment multifaceted, it's no less clear that fearful injury is traceable to those patterns, and that knowledge of the injury is indispensable to efforts at understanding and rectifying the nation's fundamental race problems.

There's nothing recondite about this knowledge: many whose roles in the 1960s were small and unheroic learned quickly at least a portion of what Moses and other Movement leaders knew. (In that decade the present writer taught young black Mississippians who were about to enter integrated schools for the first time, introducing them to their new textbooks. Few pupils had ever seen a schoolbook with illustrations; some were from counties that spent, according to public record, as little as one dollar on the education of blacks for every hundred dollars spent on the education of whites; the results of the inequities were chillingly evident.)

Furthermore, an extensive public record documents the force, over centuries, of the resistance—or, in late-twentieth-century terms, the "oppositional mental-

ity"—referred to by caste theorists. We have numberless accounts of uprisings against slavery—shipboard
insurrections (the *Dolphin,* the *Don Carlos,* the *Ferrers,*
the *Little George,* many more) and mainland revolts
(led by Solomon, Martin, and Gabriel, slaves of Thomas
Prosser, by Denmark Vesey and David Walker and Nat
Turner and many more) that culminated in the Civil
War. We have full accounts as well of the postwar struggle that began when the promises of emancipation were
broken and that at length enlisted hundreds of thousands of blacks in a movement against the white
majority.

On the face of things it seems improbable that the
cumulative weight of the documented historical injury
to African Americans could ever be lightly assessed, or
that wide assent could ever be given to the ahistorical
premise that a simple change from ill will to goodwill
within the majority would suffice to cancel the effects of
that injury. (No need for a "civil rights movement" or
extended court battles or legislative campaigns.) But
over the last decade and a half nonscholarly cultural
production has conducted a siege on the pertinent
past—systematically excising knowledge of the continuity and psychosocial consequences of this country's
historical exploitation of African Americans. And, not
surprisingly, this turn of events has sharply increased—
among enlightened whites—the plausibility of the versions of black-white sameness and harmony touted by
friendship orthodoxy.

The historical excisions occur in factitious renderings of the American past—mass entertainments that blur the outlines of black-white conflict, redefine the ground of black grievances for the purpose of diminishing the grievances, raise doubt that the grievances were ever deeply felt, and restage black life in accordance with the arbitrary and illusory conventions of American success mythology.

The topics treated include slavery, the Civil War, and the Civil Rights Movement, and the dominant themes include, in addition to the ephemerality of the human injury stemming from slavery, the insignificance of slavery as a political issue. The revisions delete power relations and the structural realities of caste from the American past. They present the operative influences on race history as the same as those implied to be pivotal in *White Men Can't Jump* or the Brooklyn Union Gas salute to Dr. King: personal attitudes and feelings. And they increase the persuasiveness of sameness and sympathy orthodoxy in two ways: first, by denying both the facts of injury and the truth that the nature of relations between blacks and whites ever emerged as a major public issue; second, by affirming that the black cause—i.e., easing the (basically minor) troubles of African Americans—has been from the start a joint project of blacks and whites.

Here is a summary of the view of the past shaping the cultural material in question:

Race history in the United States should be seen as in essence a moral drama, and the principal conflict therein isn't between a bottom caste and top caste, one black the other white, but between good and evil within the white majority. Down through the decades an ignorant, foul-natured, white-skinned criminal class—slave catchers and traders, mean masters and overseers, Klansmen, lynch mobs, bus burners, church bombers, and their ilk—committed terrible crimes. The physical suffering these fringe malefactors inflicted upon helpless blacks can't be exaggerated. Nor can it be said that enlightened whites moved with sufficient dispatch to control the rogue and hoodlum element in their midst. Often individual whites were overly preoccupied with their own concerns or inclined to luxuriate in extended bouts of conscience before making personal commitments to justice. Conceivably, the full moral resources of the community might never have been summoned had it not been for the prodding of an impressive spiritual leader, Dr. Martin Luther King.

Yet, happily, the revisionist narrative continues, enlightened whites did at length make the vital commitments. Facing down brute hatred and mindless viciousness, the responsible element provided support, friendship, sympathy, and leadership for the black cause—and, as a result, right came to prevail. Yet more happily, the spirit of African Americans—the resourceful individualism (personal pluck, drive, ambition) that stamps them as it does every American—wasn't broken, despite the physical punishment some were obliged to endure.

The revisionist narrative makes space for a few sadnesses and ambiguities, to be sure. It acknowledges that a culture with fringe group hatred and lunacy on its margins, even though in the distant past, should not engage in moral preening. But it worries that people will tear themselves apart in an excess of self-laceration. Against great odds a victory for human reason and for the fraternity of blacks and whites of goodwill—the caring majority—was wrested from suffering. Those who hold that a special providence guides the United States may well be justified in finding support for that view not only in the nation's comparative abundance and prosperity but in the remarkable tale of human aspiration and indomitableness compressed in the phrase "up from slavery."

The "historical" foundations of friendship orthodoxy lie in this story, and the distortions and caricatures of reality embodied in the tale are apparent wherever the substance of history survives. Chattel bondage was no outrage perpetrated by a wicked, hate-filled fringe. It was (as thinkers from W. E. B. Du Bois to Bob Moses were fully aware) a well-organized, durable, wealth- and power-generating socioeconomic system by which the top caste in the West adapted to and extracted gain from a particular set of historical circumstances. The chief damage done by this bondage, moreover, resulted not from the slave master's lash itself but from the dehumanization, carried out for practical purpose, of ten to fifteen generations of bottom-caste African Americans. And credit for ending slavery (and the succeeding institutions of white supremacy) belongs far less to friendly whites than to blacks who escaped the disablement of contrived inferiority and bore the lion's share of the risk and cost of the struggle.

But counterassertion in this vein is comparatively impotent. Historically oriented cultural production in support of friendship orthodoxy consists of shows—performance entertainment—not of flatly expressed propositions that can be weighed, tested against evidence, and (where appropriate) refuted. The chief individual creations—works such as the docudrama *Roots* (1977), the Ken Burns PBS series *The Civil War* (1990), big-budget films such as *Mississippi Burning* (1988) and small-budget films such as *The Long Walk Home* (1990), and nearly a dozen television biographical specials (on Dr. King, Robert Kennedy, Thurgood Marshall, Morris Dees, and others)—are closely related and compose a kind of pop epic narrative of race in America. Each builds its case dramatically, eschewing preceptorial modes. And each foregrounds emotions, gestures, and speech that add to the credibility of consensus orthodoxy while shading noncorroborative detail into shadows.

The vital link between this orthodoxy and pseudo-

and antihistory was forged, in *Roots*, with the creation of the figure of the Unscathed Slave. (Arguably the rise of the orthodoxy commenced, in fact, with this invention.)

Nominated for thirty-three Emmy Awards, the series intimated, to a seemingly enthralled audience of over 130 million, that the damages resulting from generations of birth-ascribed, semianimal status were largely temporary, that slavery was a product of motiveless malignity on the social margins rather than of respectable rationality, and that the ultimate significance of the institution lay in the proof, implicit in its defeat, that no force on earth can best the energies of American Individualism.

As presented in the show, the slave system was at once cruel and weak. *Roots* acknowledged that torture by the lash or by amputation of limb was common, and that slave families were repeatedly and heartlessly torn apart, and that some anguished whites in the slave trade knew themselves to be sinking into ever deeper corruption and degradation. Abiding by the precepts of showbiz "fairness," the production sought to awaken sympathy for pain and trials endured by blacks *and* whites in a sealed-off time past.

But what *Roots* most strenuously insisted upon was indomitability—the triumphant resurgence of the winningly individual African American, and by implication the trifling import for human development of the centuries-old caste system. As represented in the tale of the family of the maimed Kunta Kinte, chattel bondage connects nowhere with the shaping, by coercion, of a mass workforce valuable only insofar as its capacity to think, reason, and imagine an independent identity and dignity could be set under tight restraints. The history of slavery was no matter of iron stratification; deprivation of skills, opportunity, hope, and education; destruction of self-esteem; and forced adoption and transmission of defensive, outside-the-mainstream codes and strategies of survival.

To the contrary: the history of slavery was the story of a succession of generations passing through purely physical torments that left them intellectually and psychologically untouched. At the end, extricated by their own intrepid, inextinguishable shrewdness, possessed of land, means, independence, and an assured future, the undaunted children of caste cried out joyously to their forebears, announcing through the voice of Chicken George that the whole of their humanity remained intact: "Hear me, Kunta. . . . Hear me, ol' African. . . . The flesh of your flesh has come home to freedom. And you is free at last. . . . And so are we!"

Friendship orthodoxy battens, as we've seen, on faith in black-white sameness, and no barrier to interracial sameness has been, in any culture, more insurmountable than long-term imprisonment at the bottom of a rigid caste system—the historical experience and legacy of peonage. *Roots* removed that barrier. It "proved" that, thanks to native wit and doggedness, African Americans entered mainstream America wholly unscathed, "just like us." "What 'Roots' gets at," said Alex Haley, the originator (the author stepped forward in his own person in the show's final episode), is "how alike we human beings all are when you get down to the bottom, beneath these man-imposed differences we set one between the other." Promos described the series's hero as "a young man everybody could identify with."

Predictably this presentation of instant sameness—this insistence on the feasibility of an overnight rise to "equality" after centuries of purposefully dehumanized caste existence—roused objections from historians. One writer commented sardonically on the resemblance between the themes of *Roots* and those of long-running television epics about whites. "The central theme," wrote Columbia Professor Eric Foner, is "the ability of a family, through unity, self-reliance, and moral fortitude, to face and overcome adversity. Much like the Waltons confronting the depression, the family in 'Roots' neither seeks nor requires outside help; individual or family effort is always sufficient." The family inhabits the timeless, contextless, never-never land of can-do, and this necessarily narrow focus precludes, as Foner remarked, "any attempt to portray the outside world and its institutions."

The absence of the outside world, together with the presence of whites shown to have suffered from their participation in slave trading and of blacks who invincibly survived, substantially diminished black grievance. It kept slaveholding in focus as a heinous individual act in which economic gains for whites and moral and other injuries to blacks could be accurately totaled up within the space of a discrete lifetime or two. It kept slaveholding out of focus as a system of power relations from which, long after the system's formal ending, large profit for whites and large losses for blacks accrued (and continue to accrue). Profit and loss—the debts incurred and never acknowledged by whites—receded into an indistinct yesterday. Elbowing the past into nothingness, the success story set personal relations at center stage (personal relations between Chicken George and the 130 million), and proved that each black lived within the majority myth, dreamed the same dreams, took the same chances—had effortlessly become, in short, quite some time ago, one of us.

Chapter 9

The Issueless War and the Movement That Never Was

Responding to the *Roots* message ("how alike we human beings all are"), and to the newly common sight of nondestitute blacks, white audiences by the tens of millions drew closer to the minority. They experienced the hitherto "natural" gap between themselves and black people as artificial and without base, and found their own suspicions of difference and resentment quieted by the touching revelation of common humanity.

But for some a nagging problem remained: where exactly did the war—the Civil War—fit in? *Roots* circled this subject, adopting a hands-off approach both to the war and to the politics of protest that led up to it. Nowhere did the series show African Americans engaged, in number, as a movement, in moral, intellectual, or physical combat with whites. Nothing in any episode cast friendship orthodoxy in doubt by reminding audiences of how unlike "we human beings" become when divided over centuries into oppressors and oppressed.

Yet schools still taught that half a million had been killed in a war fought over the issue of whether black human beings were less human than white human beings. Understood in these terms, as the climax of a long campaign against slavery, the war told strongly against effort to downplay injury to blacks and underscore black-white sameness. And academic historians themselves insisted on the link between the war and injury to blacks. By the midtwentieth century, the profession had almost unanimously rejected explanations that sought to marginalize the issue of slavery or to present the conflict as a family feud or dispute about competing political theories. (Henry Bamford Parkes in *The American Experience*, 1947: "It was slavery, and slavery alone, that finally made it impossible for [the North and South] to remain permanently within the same federal union.") And thereafter a series of researchers followed the lead of W. E. B. Du Bois—among them Vincent Harding, David Montgomery, Eric Foner, and David Donald—documented black insurrections that led up to the war (and didn't end with emancipation).

Little in *Roots,* to repeat, disturbed audiences with allusions either to the long-term effects of slavery as an institution or to slavery as the cause of the war; nothing in the show undercut optimism about easy, overnight rapport between blacks and whites. But in the world of learning—not excluding "required" high school classes in American history—such reminders were frequent and constituted a threat of a sort to the foundations of sameness and sympathy dogma.

The threat was eased over time not by conspiracy but by cultural production better tuned to sympathy dogma than to academic history. The eleven-hour PBS series entitled *The Civil War* went beyond downscaling black injury to sever relations between slavery and the Civil War, suggesting that slavery and the war had next to no connection. Popular and much praised, the project made incidental, sequestered reference to uprisings against slavery by slaves and freedmen—the agitation that energized the abolitionist cause and helped drive Abraham Lincoln to a transforming national vision of equality and freedom. *The Civil War* also commented briefly on slavery, by displaying a famous period photograph of the scarred back of a beaten slave.

But, like *Roots,* the series bypassed the moral and economic realities of profit, power, and dehumanization that molded the slave system as a sociopolitical phenomenon and that were bound up in the conflict between the North and the South. It told its story mainly through atomistic personal testimony—voice-over snippets of individual experience from diaries and letters clean of interpretative generalizations. (The technique jibed perfectly with the bent of new thinking toward personalizing and miniaturizing.) And, most important, the eleven programs treated slavery as an irrelevancy, pressing the message that the war was a family feud, that nothing blocked compromise except demented stubbornness on both sides, and that no general ideas of substantial moral or political weight figured at the center of the conflict.

The production's favored spokesperson, Shelby Foote, opined in the opening episode that the war was pointless and wasteful—an "enormous catastrophe." And thereafter he argued—in unacknowledged contradiction of the best current scholarship—that most Northerners were latent abolitionists and that Lincoln signed the Emancipation Proclamation for no reason except to encourage Northerners to continue the fight.

Historians protested once more, rejecting *The Civil War* as—in the words of Washington University professor Jean Attie—"hackneyed" and "morally bankrupt." They drew attention to the evidence that through nearly three centuries blacks had tried to fight their oppressors—and that their oppression did indeed claim regard as a central cause of the Civil War. They pointed out that although the black drive for freedom and equality didn't end with emancipation, the dream of emancipation had inspired it from the beginning; they argued, further, that dismissive treatment of this truth trivialized the struggle that lent solemn meaning to the war and that launched a crusade whose goals remain unreached to this day. How could Shelby Foote and Ken Burns treat Bedford Forrest, founder of the Ku Klux Klan and a man who declared that he would shoot any black taken prisoner, as merely another genial old Southern gentleman?

By "implicitly denying the brutal reality of slavery," Attie wrote, the series crossed "a dangerous moral threshold"; in shrugging off emancipation, it stripped itself of credibility "even as a fair rendering of the limited terrain it covers."

But this was shoptalk—in-house, professional commentary appearing in learned journals, reaching the eyes of few of the millions who had watched and listened as the abolition of slavery was refashioned into insignificance. On its first showing and in reruns *The Civil War* won huge acclaim. Authoritative political voices certified its value. The secretary of defense sent tapes of the programs to the general directing the Gulf War. The programs' creator was invited to the White House, introduced to the queen of England, hailed as a kind of American moral exemplar at the National Press Club. And as the once earthshaking insurgency against white America—the struggle of an enslaved caste for the humanity denied them by the majority culture—slid into deeper darkness, the themes of friendship orthodoxy seemed to stand forth as almost unchallengeable.

The reason for this was that *The Civil War* deleted from sight the strongest piece of historical evidence documenting the falseness of those themes. The crux of friendship orthodoxy—key both to its decency and to its wrongheadedness—is faith in black-white mutuality and essential sameness. The strongest evidence that the country did not share this faith was the national repudiation of it that occurred almost immediately after the Civil War. In the post-Reconstruction era, America set its institutions firmly against the idea of black-white mutuality. It's a matter of historical record that the country fought a long and appallingly costly war about whether the black race was totally different from and absolutely inferior to the white. It's also a matter of historical record that, barely a decade after that war, the country came down on the side of those who scorned the notion that blacks and whites shared human dignity equally, and that it remained on this side for the better part of a century thereafter. These facts constitute weighty reasons for rejecting friendship orthodoxy as fantasy.

Ken Burns's *The Civil War* swept the facts from sight. It treated slavery, birth-ascribed inferiority, and the denial of dignity as matters of no magnitude. Blacks, not whites, had lived for centuries as slaves: this and the intensity of the national commitment to believing in their inferiority argued profoundly against easy sentimental deletion of differences between the races. The television series virtually ignored both the centuries of bondage and the national commitment, and in so doing helped to place the themes of the new thinking beyond challenge.

From America's first days as a nation, great minds had wrestled, privately and publicly, with the agonizing issue of black "inferiority." Thomas Jefferson posed the pertinent questions clearly. Are blacks, he asked, "on a par with ourselves?" Is their "want of talents . . . merely the effect of their degraded condition" or does it proceed from "difference in the structure of the parts on which intellect depends?" Slavery had lain at the heart of Southern pride in regional difference: "Southerners came to see the institution of slavery," wrote Daniel Boorstin, "as the lifeblood of all social good, nourishing the peculiar virtues of political, social, economic, and cultural life in the South." Central to that self-idealizing vision was the conception of the slave as subhuman—as a creature in need of the firm parental guidance that only a culture committed to humane (as opposed to commercial-industrial) values could provide.

And central to Lincoln's belief in the fundamental rightness of the war was the conviction that this self-idealizing vision—the fantasy that represented slavery as an adjunct of the highest freedom—would, if spread farther into the territories, utterly destroy the moral fabric of the nation. The identity of the slave, the nature of his difference, the question whether those who treated him as subhuman were or weren't morally superior to those who claimed to regard him as an equal penetrated every aspect of nineteenth-century American life—politics and governance, property and other law, labor relations, production and consumption, the high arts and the popular arts.

But hour by hour *The Civil War*, watched rapturously by educated millions, pushed slavery, caste stratification, and the political, social, and moral ramifications of the combat further to the margins of its story. Instead of directing attention to the forces increasingly differentiating the industrial and pastoral economies of the North and South—forces of signal impact on the illiterate black population—the series made light of these differences, presenting North and South as more or less the same. ("America in 1861," said the narrator in the first episode and again in the last, consisted of "31 million people [living] peaceably on farms and in small towns.")

Instead of drawing the audience close to the struggle against slavery long waged by blacks themselves, instead of helping viewers to grasp the influence of that struggle on Lincoln's own ultimate conception of the war, the series repeatedly deprecated contentions that the war was about "human dignity." (When discussing, on camera, the meaning of the conflict, Shelby Foote declared that he saw no meaning; the war was pointless.) Instead of clarifying the immediate legacy of the war—the brief period of successful battles by blacks and their allies for civil rights—the series entirely omitted mention of Reconstruction, dealt with the restoration of white supremacy as a minor irony, laid heaviest emphasis on pictures of Confederate and Union soldiers rejoicing in each other's company at reunions, pressing home that the essential story was of needless family rupture followed by reconciliation.

An opportunity to educate a mass audience in the truth that the Civil War amounted to more than an extended period of senseless bloody battles was beyond price or valuing. The PBS series could have served as the means by which the facts of black-white caste difference were brought fully to life, for the American public, after thirty years of sponsored evasion; television could have shown the nation that the war marked the beginning—but no more than that—of the advance of the oppressed slave population toward freedom and equality.

In the event, however, the series did nothing of the sort. Its creator explained, in 1990, speaking to a group of historians who asked him why slavery had been so slighted, that any discussion of slavery "would have been lengthy and boring." It would also, of course, have been discomforting—a jarring rebuke to the thesis that nothing substantial now separates blacks and whites. Delivering no rebuke, the series perfectly served the interests of contemporary orthodoxy. As we are today, so were we yesterday: sympathetic friends, taking our chances as we must, all (save for the obnoxious but now tamed racist fringe) in the same boat.

*   *   *

Revamping the history of the Civil Rights Movement in order to make *it* accommodate themes of black-white unity, sameness, and sympathy looks on its face to be a project rather more fantastic even than that of deleting slavery from the historical context of the Civil War. Half the country's living citizens remember the Movement— know it was a near-continuous battle, waged by blacks against whites, about power and its distribution. Many are also aware that the conflict originated in historic reversals of the promises of emancipation, that it was usually the respectable Establishment (mayors, police chiefs, town fathers, vestrymen, golf club boards, men of the Rotary, Kiwanis, and Lions) who led opposition to the black cause, and that (because of the legacy of injury reaching from the past) it had been difficult for black leaders to kindle and nourish political will in bottom-caste brothers and sisters. Was it conceivable that dramatizations could be hit upon that would marginalize rights issues in the Movement years as *The Civil War* marginalized slavery?

It's indicative of national dedication to sameness and sympathy themes that plotlines accomplishing that end were designed with ease. The history of the Movement became a tale of Establishment whites battling on the side of blacks against racist crazies: two races joining in mutual sacrifice and love. One film—*Mississippi*

Burning (1988)—actually went far beyond this; it transformed the civil rights struggle from a conflict pitting blacks against white society into an intra-FBI conflict about investigative methodology.

As the script had it, three people had once been abducted and murdered down South, victims of Ku Klux Klan crazies, whereupon the FBI seized the initiative. But the agents on the case (Willem Dafoe and Gene Hackman) differed philosophically about how to proceed. Dafoe was a by-the-book operative, a stickler for correct "Bureau procedures." Hackman was less bureaucratic, a frontier type aware that, when dealing with KKK gang weirdos, terror and bribery might be required. The agents dueled with each other on this issue, while risking their lives—routine conduct for white officialdom—to protect black people from the KKK crazies. ("What's *wrong* with these [Klan] people?" asked the perplexed Dafoe after the crazies launched a ferocious assault on blacks.)

In the end the nonbureaucratic approach prevailed, the guilty were apprehended, rights problems and inequities were adroitly and permanently resolved, and the nature and scale of the insurgency against the white Establishment remained out of sight.

In real life both the scale of protest and the reasons for it had been, of course, manifest. The three victims of the actual events to which the movie intermittently alluded—one black man (James Chaney) and two white men (Andrew Goodman and Michael Schwerner)—

were in the South together with hundreds of volunteers in a political cause (the attempt by the black Student Nonviolent Coordinating Committee to create a black political party capable of challenging the state's all-white Democratic regulars). The victims had trained for their work in out-of-state institutes directed by black leaders, including the legendary Bob Moses. During the five years preceding these institutes, activist leaders of the disenfranchised black minority had protested the denial of their right to register, vote, use public facilities, and organize politically. The leaders traveled farmhouse to farmhouse in the backcountry, explaining their goals, exhorting their people. Word of this effort spread nationally, and some whites—ministers, lawyers, college students—volunteered to help. The white Establishment from local to national levels sought to break the Movement, going so far as to promise—implicitly—exemption from punishment to any who did violence on the activists. (J. Edgar Hoover, Freedom Summer, 1964: "We most certainly do not and will not give protection to civil rights workers.") But despite intense pressure and much governmental evasion and waffling, the Movement did not collapse.

A once wholly familiar story. African Americans in great numbers participated in the insurgency called the Movement. Conflicting group interests within their ranks, and divergent opinions about tactics, strategy, and overall goals were negotiated day by day from top leadership levels to the streets and courthouse steps—by

American men and women who, without benefit of elite education, chose roles as activist citizens, mastered under fire the disciplines of collective, nonviolent action, and risked much for a cause they saw as just. The notion that any truth about this undertaking could be told through a story that put the Movement in charge of two white FBI agents and reduced its issues to a quarrel about police methodology ranks as extreme intellectual dishevelment.

But like *Roots* and *The Civil War, Mississippi Burning* was a contribution not to understanding of the interracial past but to the support of the new positive mind-set regarding black-white fraternity. Ignoring fact, it presented a long-running struggle between disenfranchised blacks and the majority white culture as a heartwarming episode of interracial unity; the speed and caringness of white response to oppression of blacks demonstrated that broadscale race conflict was inconceivable. The U.S. government does not tolerate redneck gangs that harass black people; the U.S. government unhesitatingly sets at risk the lives of its investigative forces in order to protect black people who cannot protect themselves; the U.S. government *led* the crusade for justice for African Americans: these were the movie's core statements.

And when smaller government entities, state or local, found themselves intimidated by redneck nuts and were slow to act—so ran the burden of other film versions of (and biographical specials about) Movement history—individual whites themselves heroically took up the moral slack. The historical focus of *The Long Walk Home* (1990), a film professedly about the Montgomery bus boycott, obliged the camera to glance at least briefly at black grievances. At the start of the movie we see black passengers entering a bus at the front to pay their fares, then exiting, reentering at the side door, and taking up their assigned space at the rear.

But the political substance of the Montgomery bus boycott swiftly disappears, its place taken by the story of a burgeoning friendship between a white matron (Sissy Spacek) and a black maid (Whoopi Goldberg), and of a quarrel that this friendship provokes between the matron and her husband. Spacek, the film's point-of-view character, is at first aware of the boycott only as an inconvenience; it obliges her to pick up her maid across town on days when she needs the woman's services early. Gradually Spacek learns that Goldberg is personally committed to the boycott. At length, moved by friendship and admiration for Goldberg, Spacek defies her husband and risks her own safety by driving for the black carpool. ("I'm with the carpool. Y'all going downtown?" "Yes, ma'am.") Whereupon the grateful Goldberg prays with her family for her heroic white friend. ("Lord, I ask you please to watch over my Mrs. Helen Thompson. I got my reasons.")

As in every other engagement in Movement history,

power and its distribution were the issues in the Montgomery boycott, blacks against whites (not white hus-
bands against white wives) were the chief contending
forces, and the rousing human story was the effort by
black leaders to sustain political will and courage
among their historically injured, caste-depressed fol-
lowers. Fifty thousand black people achieved and maintained solidarity against the white majority for longer
than a year in this uprising; the boycott involved hundreds of vehicles, dozens of pickup stations, endless re-
scheduling arrangements. The boycott leaders held to
their course through uncounted, maddening negotiating
sessions with the city's power structure and in the face
of much majority-condoned violence; whites played no
leadership role on their side.

But little or none of this turns up in the film—which
is to say that *The Long Walk Home* functions throughout as an emollient, smoothing over the history of grievance and collective political action aimed at ending
grievance, and deleting every trace of fact that might
compromise one-on-one orthodoxy or otherwise bring
to mind—after the film's first few seconds—the reality
of historical injury. The movie's tripartite message is
that white-black friendship in the time of troubles was
an all-powerful bond (like that between, for example,
Chicken George and white audiences in *Roots*); that
whites who became aware of injustice suffered by their
black friends identified totally with those friends, sacri-

ficing without stint; and that, thanks to that sacrifice, injustice and inequality—all that might stand as a barrier to black-white sameness—has been banished for good.

The ease with which pop history structured by friendship orthodoxy has succeeded in reading grievance and social struggle out of the past is partly explained by the event which, as I said at the start, conditions all the new thinking surveyed in these chapters: the emergence of a visible black middle class. But other factors were in play, and especially significant among them was the weakening of the historical sense itself—including, perhaps, the feeling for stagnancy. Imagining the weight—the deep encrustation—of centuries' old caste habit and belief demands a measure of familiarity with the experience of immobility over tracts of time; since the midnineteenth century, rapid rates of social and psychosocial change have spared much of white America that experience.

But the reasons for the persuasiveness of the message of black-white solidarity count far less than the message's ultimate impact. The combination of friendship orthodoxy and pop historical fantasy appears to have eradicated from the national consciousness the two basic truths of race in America, namely that because of what happened in the past, blacks and whites cannot yet be the same and that, because what happened in the past was no mere matter of ill will or insult—it was a matter of caste structures that have only very recently begun to be dismantled—it is not reparable by affirmative civility or one-on-one goodwill.

The assault on history encourages belief that two centuries of labor bondage followed by a century of postemancipation repression had no consequences to speak of; that the bondage caused no permanent injury; that the white majority, after momentary obliviousness, leaped in to right all existing wrongs; and that, because of this demonstrated concern, fraternal feeling must swell in every right-minded heart, black or white.

In the public that has ingested either a part or the whole of this revisionism the word "slavery" has come to induce stock responses (Massa, the mansion house, spirituals, the Underground Railway, and so on), with no vital sense of a grinding devastation of mind occurring generation upon generation. Duped by superficial knowingness, otherwise decent men and women commence to ignore the past, or to summon for it a detached, correct "compassion," or to gaze at it as though it were a set of aesthetic conventions, like twisted trees and fragmented rocks in nineteenth-century picturesque painting—lifeless phenomena without bearing on the present. The possibility of striking through the mask of corporate-underwritten, feel-good, historyless, racism-is-silly consensus thought grows daily more remote. And with the disappearance of the past, the race crises of the present grow ever more baffling and impenetrable—even, finally, meaningless.

*   *   *

Our anatomy of the enlightened mind-set is nearly complete, but a few unfinished matters remain. I have argued that successes in rewriting the past in accordance with friendship orthodoxy have eased the enlightened white conscience, opening useful escape routes from blame. But the severest challenge to the psychology of blamelessness is mounted not by the past but by the here and now—by the sights and sounds of immediate daily experience. No satisfactory inquiry into current ways of thinking about race can avoid the question of how enlightened minds deal with that challenge.

How is it possible to sustain faith in sameness and sympathy between the races when one knows at first hand the texture of today's American cityscape—the ocular evidence that gives the lie to versions of black America as solidly middle class? What are the sequences of thought and feeling that enable men and women neither callous nor credulous to confront, day after day, in their lived experience, manifest inequity while clinging to the myth of sameness and escaping altogether the sense of personal misconduct? Among the most troubling content of the contemporary mind-set is that which holds answers to these questions.

Chapter 10

Clearing the
Conscience (I):
The Mystique of Can-Do

In urban America belief in black-white sameness would seem hard to sustain. The ineluctable facts—the look of the streets, wretched housing conditions, the predominance of blacks among homeless men and women, the sight of pregnant black children—chide fantasy, mock the inanities of friendship dogma's formulary optimism. "I have counted," writes the distinguished critic Alfred Kazin, "I have counted four and five [black] beggars to a block, block after block, on the streets of the Upper West Side in New York. You cannot walk without being afflicted, and you are spiritually worse off if you manage to pass unscathed."

The observation suggests that men and women in middle- and upper-middle-class Manhattan walk their neighborhoods with pained consciences, understanding that "to pass unscathed" is to incur a different kind of wound. The walkers are aware, both at home in their buildings and in the workplace, that four or five beggars to an Upper West Side block stand for a significant moral and numerical reality—for masses of human lives, close at hand in every direction, sunk in despair. White walkers in the city, says the critic, feel that despair.

Yet for the most part they bear the torment stoically.

Several well-studied forces lie behind the stoicism—urban anonymity, faith that the worthy will at length rise (the national ethos of individualism and social mobility), politically inspired misassessments of the size and pace of expansion of the black middle class. A further, relatively unstudied force fending off the affliction—the implied arraignment—of street life, is the steady supply, by the media, of evidence indicating that, step by step, the hard problems are being solved.

In newspapers and on television the account of black crime is, of course, unrelenting, but only a little less so is the reporting on public-spirited white effort to be of service to blacks. Good news is moved throughout the day in sound, pictures, and print; nearly every broadcaster and publisher adds to the annealing flow.

147

Testifying almost uninterruptedly to the variety of current, on-line, ameliorative enterprises, the media feed strengthens the illusion that such initiatives can nullify the surrounding social context, clearing pure space for equity. The feed nowhere alters poverty rates or the beggar count, but it does tune minds to fortifying notes of hope.

And, since the feed consists largely of tales of white goodness and activism, it provides a quantity of agreeable moral stroking: stories of pro bono efforts by white Americans to speed the advance of black Americans, accounts of projects wherein corporations and/or advantaged individual citizens "give of themselves instead of giving money," testimony establishing that in wealthy enclaves without a minority presence the citizenry nevertheless remains mindful of the less fortunate. The underlying ahistorical assumptions are everywhere leveraged by friendship orthodoxy, but close examination of the upbeat feed establishes that it is no mere auxiliary; it exerts its own distinctive influence on the enlightened mind-set.

Here for example is a recent issue of "Education Life," the Sunday *New York Times* supplement on schools. The editorial tone is set in a warm and friendly headnote to a quiz feature about Bangladesh, Zimbabwe, Soweto, Idi Amin, Desmond Tutu, Julius Nyerere, other figures and places. "The global village being what it is," says the note, "Americans have become familiar, if not exactly cozy, with neighbors and neighborhoods thousands of miles away. Soweto and Managua, Chamorro and Bhutto, Mugabe and Mubarak—these names, often mistaken for exotic spices just a few years ago, today elicit nods that say, 'I know you, read about you, saw you on TV.' Now you just have to place them, when they entered your life and your living room, and why. After all, it's the neighborly thing to do.''

Thereafter in "Education Life" can-do takes command. The section's lead piece salutes Chicago's Board of Education for realizing that "the city schools needed a hand, not a handout." The board instituted an Adopt-a-School program for which new hands are constantly volunteering. A Chicago law firm recently turned its thirty-odd partners into mentors, each working with a minority student for ninety minutes a week, all revealing a flexible readiness to adapt goals to persons.

"Paula Goedert, a [law] partner, said she initially decided to improve her student's reading skills. 'After the first three weeks I realized that she wasn't going to be a super reader in ten weeks,' Ms. Goedert said. 'So I changed my goal—to make her more confident.' Sterling Milan [a sixth-grader in the program] said that he and his lawyer-mentor 'wrote a book—on a legal pad—about a boy who grew up on a farm.' ''

Turn the page. Rochester, New York, has a new "child associates" program that targets "school adjustment problems before they become dropout realities." Nonprofessional "child associates" work with endangered kindergarten through third-grade kids for twenty minutes twice a week; the associates "apply warmth, genuineness, trust and the ability to share," "play games with the youngsters, trying to determine the nature of the problems and to help them resolve it." The effort "translates to essentially healthy children." "If you're not feeling any kind of pain or suffering," the supervising elementary school principal observes, "I think you're going to do better in school."

Harlem, says "Education Life," has a new Law and Social Problems high school project created by Legal Outreach Inc. (Legal Outreach is "a nonprofit organization that provides legal services"; the organization believes that "there are a lot of bright and talented students in Harlem" and that "all they need is an opportunity.") A student-run mock trial competition is planned—to be judged by a panel of city judges ("students considering a legal career may be paired with lawyer mentors"). The long-range goal is "to provide students with the knowledge and information to help them evaluate and improve the quality of life in their communities."

Students discuss in class an imaginary police roundup and search, for drugs, without permission, of six teenagers, five with drug records. (The latter five prove to have drugs in their pockets.) The discussion clarifies that in these situations there is no one villain.

"The police were undoubtedly wrong?" Ms. Foy [the teacher] asked.

"Yes," the class resounded.

"And the boys were undoubtedly right?"

"It was fifty-fifty," blurted Carlos Roman, a fifteen-year-old. "They violated the kids' rights by going through their pockets without asking."

Ms. Foy nodded. "The police cannot go on hunches. They have to have a legitimate reason to believe that someone committed a crime."

Carlos Roman speaks excitedly about the course to *The Times*'s reporter, declaring proudly that now he knows his rights: "I know what I can do and what I can't do."

Texas is working with parents as well as with students, according to another feature. A Dallas program "coaches parents especially in immigrant and minority neighborhoods to teach their young children at home simple skills like shapes, colors and listening." Kent Tucker, "a pressman in the Dallas public schools print shop and a single parent of four, ages three through six," says the program has "improved the hand coordination of his daughter Keoshia, age four."

Scarsdale, New York, is making its own contributions. A profile of an admired history teacher in that town's high school notes that the school has unparalleled resources (good salaries, small classes, high community esteem for faculty, much encouragement and reward for ambitious, achieving students). But more impressive still is that the devoted and gifted teacher who is profiled has his own special program for the less fortunate. He "remains deeply committed, as he has been for twenty years, to a program to bring black students from the South to Scarsdale for their junior and senior years. Many of those students, he says, have gone on to top colleges."

Miami Beach is on the move. One system "tested all its 600 students at the start of the 1991–92 school year to determine how each one learns best, then allowed parents to pursue the route most comfortable to them."

Philadelphia is attacking its dropout problem. Until recently half the city's ninth-graders weren't promoted. "Such failure, many dropout experts assert, is so discouraging to students that many—already burdened by the harsh life of the inner city—leave school." But "now, in the second year of its three-year financing allotment, the Philadelphia model has helped raise the number of ninth graders promoted because of the additional personal attention." The key to the turnaround, the piece explains, is allowing students to work with the same team of teachers from grade nine through twelve. This cluster approach "give[s] at-risk students . . . a greater sense of place."

And so on, for the balance of the supplement's sixty pages. The movement repeated in piece after piece is from sharp definition to swift resolution. Problems are neatly sealed off from their surround; problem-solving approaches are of laserlike conclusiveness; messy entanglements of social context—the heart-dauntingly multiform exfoliations of caste history—do not obtrude.

In this confident, pop-echoing elimination of social context lies the uncommon power of the discourse. If Harlem youth experiences difficulty in daily interaction with the police, a class explaining constitutional guarantees can put things right. There's no habitat, no social climate—no possibility, that is, that youths explaining their constitutional rights to cops who address them rudely on, say, the corner of Amsterdam and 110th Street could suffer beatings before completing their projects "evaluating the quality of life of the community."

Or if the "harshness" of inner-city life discourages students, a cluster approach in senior high can put things right. Again no context: no possibility, that is, that the weight of the hood—the pupil's friends doing business in her project entryway, no supper, nowhere to work, no grown-up determined to provide quiet space and encouraging words, sometimes interference from an aunt's or cousin's snag-bent boyfriend pawing one's homework papers—may shatter "the sense of place" provided at school. If a lawyer experiences obstacles in an attempt to improve the reading skills of a ghetto child, a turn toward confidence building can put things right. The wealth and privilege made manifest in a single Scarsdale school building symbolize the maldistribution of resources troubling the larger society, but invitations to one or two black students "from the South"—exotic spices—to share the local wealth put things right. Applications of warmth, twenty minutes twice a week, put things right for hypermanic first-graders. New teaching materials put things right for an employed black father trying to raise four children under age seven without a mate.

Everywhere the thousand-points-of-light approach proclaims scattered, isolated initiatives to be far superior to concerted efforts to grapple with problems and crises that erupt simultaneously in all urban communities. Everywhere the irresistible and intoxicating energy of can-do burns off environments, creating the pure space of equity wherein lawyer-mentors and pupils finish in peace, on legal pads, their books about a boy on a farm. "Education Life" carries an article called "Holding Back to Get Ahead" that finds similarities in the situation of black children who "fail" preschool (and therefore start kindergarten under a cloud) and that of white children who are held back voluntarily—to gain academic advantage—by their well-off parents. There's a piece conveying that civil rights is a problem for suburban whites as for blacks. One teenager's school "switched field hockey coaches five times in six weeks"; to get satisfaction, parents had to organize, file briefs with the U.S. Department of Education's Civil Rights Office, enter litigation. Blacks and whites together.

It's untrue, says a piece on Jewish day schools, that urban kids in private schools are better off than those who go where schooling is free. Tuition at yeshivas can run as high as $10,000 a year, and those who pay it are buying deprivation, not advantage: "The resources the

schools can offer students, while better than a generation ago, pale by comparison to the public schools."

Private schools need a handout not a hand.

It isn't, of course, only in great metropolitan newspapers of record like *The New York Times* that the
language of can-do resounds. Straight from the White
House and House Speaker comes a prescription for
fixing what ails the minority: workfare, vocational
training, collaring deadbeat dads. Reading experts in
the academy tout this or that book as a force that
could make the difference for Harlem youth. "Internationally known consultant in education" James Moffett
opines that the autobiography of Althea Gibson is a
must: "Youngsters growing up in an environment of
despair and desperation need very much to read how
others just like themselves learned to take charge of
their lives and rise above the futile street life Gibson
recalls."

NBC Sports, Turner TV, McDonald's, and the National Basketball Association have their own handle on
the dropout problem. It's an annual "Stay in School"
scheme that gives schoolkids in each year's All-Star
Game city a satin jacket or free ticket to an exhibition,
provided the kids don't miss a schoolday in the month
of January. "Stay in School seem[s] to be the right approach," says the basketball commissioner. "Perfect at-
tendance was up 48 percent over the year before."

*   *   *

Notable differences exist between the discourse of one-on-one friendship and the discourse of can-do. Well seeded with anecdotes that hold up a mirror in which properly feeling readers or viewers can observe their own sympathy, can-do talk nevertheless centers—as indicated—on arranged interaction between the races, not on spontaneous outbursts of warm interracial feeling. And its preferred manner is objective/journalistic, not dramatic or hortatory.

But both discourses are charged with strong currents of optimism and self-appreciation. And they send an unambiguous, two-pronged, joint message: (1) vitally ameliorative forces are in play; (2) pangs of conscience are inappropriate save among whites who bear personal ill will toward the minority or have done it injury by conscious intent.

As for the question of overall impact: neither singly nor in combination can the two discourses strip street life of its capacity to wound—the silent *J'accuse.* To reach that goal, more is needed (and is supplied, as will shortly be seen). But together, easing the lingering pressures of historical remembrance as well as the observed afflictions of the present, they can mildly moderate impulses of self-reproach.

Heartening, context-erasing "reports" on points-of-light initiatives and selfless labor in the cause of African Americans hint at the possibility that the troubles of this block and the next should be understood as phenomena in transition, symptoms of an order of feelinglessness whose shameful day is ending. Whether the suggestion is made in tonight's concerned local telecast or in the morning paper, it brings easement for responsive urbanities. Edging silently past a sovereign-eyed mendicant posted near the entrance to Zabar's or H&H Bagels, or counting sidewalk homeless while walking the dog, I am not obliged (assuming that I attend to the media feed) to see myself or my fellows as uncaring neighbors of atrocity. The symptoms that catch my eye need not be read as fixed, unchanging, inevitable consequences of uncounted generations of caste existence. *At times the situation seems hopeless but still. . . . Worthwhile projects are starting up. Practical projects with modest ambitions, avoiding hysteria. Concrete, worthwhile projects. People care. The situation is mainly out of our hands. But things are going on in the neighborhoods, which is good. Neighborhoods count.*

Bottom line: some attention is being paid.

Chapter 11

Clearing the Conscience (II):
A Free Choice of Life

Either them Korean motherfuckers
are geniuses or you black asses
are just plain dumb.
—*Do the Right Thing (1989)*

The speaker of the line above is M.L., a black man who, with two companions—one of them Sweet Dick Willie, played by the late, great comedian Robin Harris—functions as chorus in the Spike Lee film. Seated under a tatty umbrella on a Brooklyn street, the three men eye a Korean grocery across the way. "Lookit those Korean motherfuckers," says M.L. "I betcha they haven't been off the boat a year before they open up their own place. Motherfucking year off the motherfucking boat and they already got a business in *our* neighborhood—a *good* business. . . . Now for the life of me, you know, I can't figure this out."

M.L.'s mocking conclusion (either Koreans are geniuses or blacks are dumb) is a detail of characterization but something else as well. In the late 1980s the maybe-blacks-are-dumb perspective was duplicated in a number of black contributions to pop—from Keenan Ivory Wayans's *In Living Color,* to Shahrazad Ali's best-selling attack on black males (*The Blackman's Guide to Understanding the Blackwoman,* 1989). And echoes of the carping came to be heard in the friendship discourse of white media, in editorial columns, foundation position papers, reports on curriculum disputes, and campus rows about free speech and "political correctness."

This critical "candor" bespoke confidence, stemming from the rise of friendship doctrines, that warmly benevolent feelings toward African Americans were universal, hence no longer needed dressing out in artificial manners—deference, flattery, and the like. The confidence was displayed across the cultural board, from editorial columns to TV sports shows claiming (as seen early in this book) that people no longer had to prove their lack of "prejudice" by insisting on the saintly, brainy nature of every member of every minority.

But there was more to the so-called candor than mere rejection of yesteryear's pious liberal preening. Again as noted earlier, castelike societies attempting to dismantle parts of their stratification systems lose patience quickly. Both the majority and the making-it minority, troubled by lack of change in the grossly disturbing elements of everyday bottom-caste experience, seek interpretations—stories—that explain slow rates of progress without attributing them either to large-scale, systemic, historical and socioeconomic factors *or* to foot-dragging on the part of elites. More than one caste-like society abroad has regressed swiftly to belief that its bottom castes suffer regrettably from ineradicable genetic defects. And talk of "black asses" as "just plain dumb" was one among many signs of similar temptations here.

This *is* America, however. The country doesn't easily give itself to public harshness. Its traditions and pieties forbid the casual shedding of sameness myths. Its can-do rhetoric and sunny tales of black-white fellowship insist on white goodwill and blamelessness. Its fantasy life reverberates with tales of blacks who are necessarily, pleasingly, overwhelmingly grateful to whites. ("I would take a bullet for you," says a black White House guard passionately to the friendly white man/quasi president in the box-office hit *Dave*, 1993.) The situation required, as I say, a formula that would permit a measure of criticism of blacks—criticism that would check up short of genetic slander and that would simultaneously reaffirm whites' earnest concern.

The formula arrived at provided an interpretation of the mix of universal white goodwill and slow black progress that was gratifyingly exculpatory. It proposed

that the reason blacks were moving ahead only halt-
ingly might be that excessive white generosity had
slowed them down. The basic problem wasn't the intellectual and educational and socioeconomic deficit piled
up during centuries of absolute race stratification. It
was, instead, the understandable but nevertheless not
finally benign disposition of softhearted white Americans to spoil their black brothers and sisters rotten.

The more mindless comment in this vein centered
on alleged overcosseted black recipients of welfare on
one hand and overindulged black leaders on the other.
Ronald Reagan told the nation about "welfare queens"
who, he had learned, drove to the post office in new
Cadillacs to pick up their government subsistence
checks. Talk-show hosts held forth on the pampering of
the Reverends Jesse Jackson and Al Sharpton. ("Those
guys," said Manhattan's Bob Grant, "wouldn't know an
honest day's work if it were presented to them, because
they live high off the hog.") Campaign managers regularly met their responsibility to produce new, particularly egregious evidence of mollycoddling. (In the 1994
Massachusetts gubernatorial race between William
Weld and Mark Roosevelt, a major issue developed from
the charge that Weld as governor had allowed millions
in welfare payments to be "illegally given to rapists and
murderers in prison.")

Denunciation of counterproductive white largesse
figured prominently in the 1994 controversy about
black intelligence. One controversialist, the white soci-

ologist Seymour Itzkoff, asserted that the "welfare system has gone a long way to destroying much . . . potential by subsidizing behaviors that we'd rather not have." At present the claim that intellectual and moral babying of blacks, by well-intentioned liberals, has effectively ruined their appetite for work has attained, in many quarters, the status of received truth.

Chief spokesmen for this thesis outside the world of pop were the young black neoconservative academics—Shelby Steele and Stephen Carter were the best known—who, like Spike Lee, came to notice in the late 1980s. Arguing that white goodwill could now be assumed and that efforts to aid African Americans through programs of racial preference caused psychological harm, these writers had a more complex agenda in mind than did the white Tories who often wrenched their words out of context. But Steele, Carter, and others did insist that the time had come to stop "coddling the minority"; they strongly urged that black individualistic energy must henceforth be required to prove itself on its own.

The position made waves. Previous preaching, by whites, against special treatment for minorities had been easy to abuse as reactionary and heartless. And the rare black writer who sided with the preaching tended to avoid direct attacks on black activist leaders and seldom addressed general audiences. Not so the new black neoconservatives. Early achievers in professional disciplines, they were seeking a wide public—and they didn't hesitate to challenge black leaders who, certain that the problems facing black America derived from historical caste reality, continued to urge new public commitments. Rightist commentators and organs of opinion praised the black neoconservatives unreservedly—"If you read no other book . . . make it Shelby Steele's," wrote George Will—and their message quickly got out.

The message of self-help and black independence gained plausibility from the evidence that some blacks were making real economic progress. And there was stunning synergy between the message and the central themes of friendship orthodoxy. Those themes are, to recapitulate, black-white sameness, the decline of racism and the advent of one-on-one interracial goodwill, and the relative inconsequence both of history and of the collectivist struggle by African Americans against the white majority. For the better part of the 1980s, cultural production elaborating on these themes had been largely white sponsored, centered in the world of pop. With the coming of black neoconservatism, the situation changed. In the work of the emerging young academicians, basic friendship themes remained pivotal, but they underwent subtle transformation and dignification. Staples of the fun culture, such as comedy and knockabout bonhomie, were banished, as was history; concepts from theology, philosophy, and psychoanalytic theory were interfused; the tone grew sterner.

Fairness demands repeated acknowledgement that a primary goal of the black neoconservatives was to put on record, fearlessly, that at least some African Americans recognized the welfare system to be not merely a failure but, because it perpetuated dependency, a blight on the hopes of their race. In pursuing that goal, however, they laid less stress on the need for new conceptions of nationally supported racial development than on the themes of black-white sameness that had come to dominate cultural life. In short, despite huge differences in tone, idiom, and ultimate purpose, pop and academic black conservatism jointly backed the attitudes and assumptions of friendship orthodoxy. And that cultural rapprochement hastened the process by which the orthodoxy established its broad claim to respectability. In the pages of the black neoconservatives it was possible to find moral, philosophical, and psychological justifications for the view that *the surest proof of white kindness and caring would be a national decision to leave blacks alone to solve their problems for themselves.* And with the triumph of this view, friendship orthodoxy reached its apogee.

The definitive black neoconservative text was Shelby Steele's *The Content of Our Character* (1990), subtitled *A New Vision of Race in America.* An English professor in the California state college system, Steele articulated his new vision in ten chapters composed in a nonmilitant, autobiographical style. He drew on his classroom knowledge of young black undergraduates, on memories of his own youth as a poor black growing up in Chicago, and on his adult experience as a suburbanite member of a secure and respected professional class.

But despite the uncontentious tone (one newspaper critic spoke of the author as "the perfect voice of reason in a sea of hate"), *The Content of Our Character* is a cunningly argued work. Structured as a series of essays redefining three key terms (power, racism, and the self), the book advances unremittingly toward its goal, namely the displacement of historical and socioeconomic factors from their once dominant position in race discourse. At one and the same time it provides new intellectual footing for the range of assumptions underlying the contemporary enlightened mind-set and defines, with passion, the grounds on which majority culture neglect of black America could now claim to be truly benign.

Black-White Sameness: The Theological Overview

Steele's approach to the matter of interracial sameness lies through analysis of power relations between the races. Pre–Shelby Steele, conventional commentary on this subject focused—when addressing the period before emancipation—on white ownership of blacks, as chattel property, during the centuries of slavery. Commentary on postemancipation power relations focused on denials to blacks, by whites, of the right to vote, receive equal protection under law, use public facilities (schools, parks, transportation), and so on. The imbalance of power between the groups was seen in clear, concrete, objective events: the punishment of slaves with thirty lashes for attempting to learn to read, or, for an example from the present, shortages of textbooks in schools attended largely by black pupils (as in the South Bronx, where members of a high school science course recently spent an entire year without texts).

The Content of Our Character takes the position that reading power relations in these terms is superficial. The events that count occur below the surface, in the psyche, and are determined by an inward calculus of innocence. *"Innocence is power,"* Steele declares in his opening chapter. "What blacks lost in power [through slavery] they gained in innocence—innocence that, in turn, entitled them to pursue power." Good sense about power relations between the races therefore demands, Steele argues, that we look beyond social circumstances (oppression and victimization) to the moral and psychological transactions that social circumstance triggers.

When we do so, we grasp that laws of compensation have always been at work in black-white relations. (Exercising the power to oppress invariably costs the oppressor; suffering oppression invariably brings gain—in the form of moral capital—to the oppressed.) The oppressed relish possession of this moral capital, relish it so intensely that they refuse to give it up even after oppression ceases. ("We [blacks] have a hidden investment in victimization and poverty. . . . One sees evidence of this in the near happiness with which certain black leaders recount the horror of Howard Beach.") And accounts of the past or present that address power differentials between the races in moral terms—base white slaveowner or landlord, necessarily pure black slave or tenant—are simplistic. A basic corruption was and still is shared, and it was consensually acknowledged, to a degree, at the very beginning. "The original sin that brought us to an impasse . . . occurred centuries ago when it was first decided [presumably slaves and slave catchers arrived at the "decision" in consultation] to exploit racial difference as a means to power."

Implicit in all this is that race difference today is a sham—a fanciful scrim curtain hiding the homely commonalities of human nature. Racial stratification simply doesn't exist, because differences in worldly power are of negligible consequence. Humankind both black and white seeks personal advantage and endures the curse of imperfection; pleasures of selfishness on one side are matched by pleasures of moral vanity and self-pity on the other; shedding allegiance to the concepts of moral and social difference is the first step toward sanity.

Pushing readers to take that step, *The Content of*

Our Character details approaches that helped the author himself advance beyond color. ("In the writing, I have had both to remember and forget that I am black. . . . I have tried to search out the human universals that explain the racial specifics.") More than once Steele denounces flat out, as precious, those who take difference seriously. ("Difference becomes inaccessible preciousness toward which outsiders are expected to be simply and uncomprehendingly reverential.") And, not trivial in rhetorical terms, Steele works the theme of essential sameness into the very rhythm and syntax of his prose, through heavy use of coordinated parallelism; sentences repeatedly balance white and black on the fulcrum of a semicolon. ("Whites gain superiority by not knowing blacks; blacks gain entitlement by not seeing their own responsibility for bettering themselves.") It's one measure of this author's clarity about his mission that his syntactical structures echo the lesson pressed in his overt lines of argument. The lesson is that, because power is innocence and original sin corrupts us all, blacks and whites are the same.

Racism and Self-Deception: The Psychoanalytic Overview

Steele introduces one-on-one themes of sympathy and goodwill via a probe of the nature of racism. And again he dissents from conventional definitions. "Before the sixties," he asserts, "race set the boundaries of black life. Now, especially for middle-class blacks, it is far less a factor, though we don't always like to admit it." Black leaders are to blame for this minority evasiveness. "Though we have gained equality under law and even special entitlements through social programs and affirmative action, our leadership continues to stress our victimization." Their dogged insistence that "white racism and racial discrimination are still the primary black problem" amounts to a knee-jerk "party line."

African Americans don't need a party line; they do need, says Steele, a fresh concept of racism—one that directs the eye away from ancient offenses of whites and toward present-day self-deceptions of blacks themselves. Steele's own fresh concept rests on a psychoanalytic theory of "denial," "recomposition," and "distortion"; it makes the term "racism" into a synonym for false charges, brought for ego-defensive purposes, by blacks ashamed of their performance in interracial encounters.

He draws a key example from an episode in his own youth. "In a nice but insistent way," a white woman, mother of one of his swimming teammates in junior high, corrects Steele's grammar and pronunciation when he lapses into black English. Steele is abashed. "I felt racial shame. .... It was as though she was saying that the black part of me was not good enough, would not do." Covering his mortification, he decides his friend's mother should be ashamed of herself—for "being racist and humiliating me out of some perverse need." And he says as much to the white teammate, telling the lad that his mother doesn't "like black people and [is] taking it out on me."

Later he learns he was wrong: the woman had grown up poor, by her own words "didn't give a 'good goddam' about my race," knew that Steele was ambitious, and had only meant to help him realize his ambitions. "My comment had genuinely hurt her . . . her motive in correcting my English had been no more than simple human kindness. . . . I converted kindness into harassment and my racial shame into her racism."

The book argues that "this sequence"—the rejection of one-on-one kindness, the racist transformation, by blacks, of white goodwill into ill will—"is one of the most unrecognized yet potent forces in contemporary black life." Everywhere blacks experience "integration shock"—eruptions of "racial doubt that come . . . in integrated situations." And instead of facing up to that doubt and shame as something to be overcome within them, they "recompose" it, "externalize [doubts and threats] by seeing others as responsible for them."

Racism thus conceived hasn't to do with the evolution of yesterday's enforced illiteracy into today's textbookless classrooms, or with the evolution of yesterday's outright bans of blacks from trades into today's job ceilings, or with the evolution of yesterday's patterns of segregation (extending from housing into all sectors of life) into today's token integration. Racism hasn't to do either with history or with caste structures or with the actions and policies of a majority reluctant to cope realistically with the consequences of history. Racism is, instead, a verbal or psychological magic practiced by blacks that renders invisible to them the truth of their own evasiveness—their own fear of not being good enough.

Redefining racism in these terms strengthens belief that history casts no useful light on race issues, and that political action in the public world achieves less in the way of solutions to race problems that can be achieved through explorations of the microworld of individual psychology (private responses, emotional intricacies). More important (considering the majority culture interest in distancing itself from anguish), the redefinition presents the persistence of anguish as itself a mode of perverse black aggression—an attempt, by blacks, to distance *themselves* from the too kind, too demanding intrusiveness of the white discourse of one-on-one. In sum: whites excessively concerned about black disabilities are *forcing* blacks to cling to those disabilities out of defensive pride.

Can-Do and Autonomy: The Existential Perspective

The subject of will and choice touched on in Steele's treatment of racism is the crux of *The Content of Our Character*—the point at which the paradox of neglect as the highest form of sympathy comes into sharp focus. The matter is most fully broached in the discussion of concepts of self, and again the discussion begins with a dissent from standard definitions.

Two ranges of meaning, personal and social, figure in standard versions of self: the self as a directing inner entity (a felt continuity of experience, a "personality") and the self as "influenced" (socially conditioned, shaped partly in reflective interaction with others). Steele's dissent rests on the belief that, for African Americans, the social self is a kind of evil tempter—an "anti-self" luring people away from their first responsibility, which is to "show *ourselves* and (only indirectly) the larger society that we are not inferior in any dimension."

Steele claims that, in African Americans, the idea of social conditioning swallows up the idea of the self as controlling agent, causing an enfeebling retreat into blackness as a sanctuary: "It is easier to be 'African-American' than to organize oneself on one's own terms and around one's own aspirations and then, through sustained effort and difficult achievement, put one's insidious anti-self quietly to rest." The anti-self or social self is irremediably defeatist; it pretends that there are no choices, and, for blacks, that pretense spells disaster.

"We can talk about the weakened black family and countless other scars of oppression and poverty," Steele writes, but none of these things "eliminates the margin of choice that remains open. Choice lives in even the most blighted circumstances." It does so because "the individual is the seat of all energy, creativity, motivation, and power." Other groups—"particularly recent immigrants from Southeast Asia"—understand this. Steele's version of can-do immigrants, like that of other black neoconservatives, totally ignores the differences of circumstance between them and African Americans (differences explored in caste scholarship). Can-do immigrants believe in "individual initiative, self-interested hard work, individual responsibility, delayed gratification." But "our leadership, and black Americans in general have woefully neglected the power and importance of these values." And the resulting weakness "has been, since the mid-Sixties, a far greater detriment to our advancement than any remaining racial victimization."

Most American tributes to the values of individualism are haunted by familiar presences from Horatio Alger to Charles Lindbergh to Oliver North—go-getters, self-starters, Maslovian self-actualizers. Steele's tribute is no exception, and he's given to moralistic chiding in Franklinesque vein. There's an indictment of black parents, for instance, for sending their children an anti-can-do, white-baiting "double message: go to school but don't really apply yourself." There's no allusion whatever to the connection between that behavior, de facto ascribed inferiority, and justifiable black hostility to abysmal school systems or to white moral self-congratulation.

Nor is there any hesitation in reaching outside the American context in building the case against African Americans. Time and again, in stories of individuals losing the energizing sense of personal identity in "black identity," and in descriptions of the collapse of the Civil Rights Movement into collectivist delusion, the author falls into existentialist fustian, invoking the language of limitless human possibility—of self-creation in total and absolute freedom, of individuals hurling themselves into the uncharted future. "Blacks must be responsible for actualizing their own lives," Steele writes. "The responsible person knows that the quality of his life is something that he will have to make inside the limits of his fate. . . . He can choose and act, and choose and act again, without illusion. He can create himself and make himself felt in the world. Such a person has power."

With the appearance of this unencumbered, uncircumscribed, unconditioned figure—the Sartrean hero, a figure well removed from Joyce Ann Moore or nearly any of several million welfare mothers and their young—Steele leaves can-do, making-it America behind and ascends to the plane of pure historylessness. His embrace of the bootstrapping existentialist creed is meant as a corrective, a political act, perhaps even as a gesture of despair at "programs" his perceptiveness recognizes as cruel evasions. But the embrace takes him beyond the end of racism and the advent of universal friendly feeling. It gives comfort to all who wish to believe that for the white majority to attempt to "do more" would be emasculating. It encourages society as a whole, every afflicted walker in the city, to recognize a new duty: that of stepping aside and allowing African Americans—in the name not merely of loving fraternity but of the sacred value of freedom—to find their inner heroism and create their autonomous selves.

A number of writers—among them Glenn Loury, Thomas Sowell, Walter Williams, Randall Kennedy, and Stephen Carter—hold equal rank with Shelby Steele as architects of black neoconservatism. (It's fair to note that not all of them prize Steele's book. In *Reflections of an Affirmative Action Baby*, 1991, for example, Stephen Carter—a young Yale law professor—complains that Steele "paints too rosy a picture of American society" even as he commends Steele for "thinking in fresh and compassionate ways.")

But from the point of view of its impact on the enlightened mind-set, *The Content of Our Character* stands alone. It was the first work addressed to a general audience that translated the main themes of friendship orthodoxy from comedy, entertainment, general gregariousness, liberal piety, and vague mysticism into cultural criticism and analytical history. It ended the disgracefully protracted silence about the uselessness of the welfare system. Under favorable circumstances it might have managed to prod white America toward morally realistic comprehension of how it had failed black America and how to rectify the failure. Although the soul of the book's message lay elsewhere, Steele himself spoke approvingly, even sometimes with unreserved enthusiasm, of "developmental assistance."

But the circumstances were not favorable. The country had been schooled for years on instant black-white sameness and unity—on interracial alley-oops and slam dunks and matched costumes (black Joseph and white Jared in Wal-Mart's French Toast swimwear), on Cosby kids and buddy-cop amity and Bobbie and Dell and the fantasy discourses of one-on-one and can-do. At their best, Shelby Steele and his like-minded colleagues were telling their countrymen a complicated truth; obeying the dictates of pride in their own achievements, they were asserting black-white equality and sameness *now* and at the same time attempting to acknowledge that, for many, equality had not been achieved and would never be achieved if present policies remained in force.

The culture listened only slackly and trivialized the complex truth—reduced it to a justification of moral truancy. And with "neoconservatism" and friendship orthodoxy joined in metaphorical unison, something akin to a single story came to be driven home at every cultural level—high, middle, and low: history can be forgotten, git-go initiative is the miracle cure, impassivity equals concern (blacks must learn to go it alone), cordiality equals concern (say a friendly hello to domestic workers and make their day), blacks and whites are one (taking equal chances, going head to head in fair competition, all in the same boat, together at last in the American mainstream).

The outlooks inspired by this story (optimistic, pessimistic, apathetic) vary along the axis from liberal to moderate to conservative. But the tragically simplistic assumptions that structure the tale seem now to have won acceptance throughout the educated and well-meaning majority. We are speaking, to repeat, of the enlightened mind-set.

Chapter 12

Conclusion:

Life After Tolerance

The introduction to this book describes friendship orthodoxy as a destructive delusion; what the delusion destroys, obviously, is common sense.

Common sense avoids preaching Emersonian individualism to people without jobs, skills, shelter, or belief in the moral authority of the preachers. Common sense acknowledges that when two thirds of a caste are ill fed, ill clothed, and ill housed, the relative well-being of the remaining third is best viewed as only imperfectly indicative of the condition of the caste as a whole. Common sense isn't afraid to describe a poor, uneducated, black woman as poor, uneducated, and black, and, when such a woman is alleged to have behaved criminally, common sense weighs the factor of helplessness in judging the woman's case. Common sense knows that goodwill in itself cannot repair social injury, and that failures of individual ambition and drive are neither the sole nor the principal cause of African American dilemmas, and that there can be no straight thinking about race without a steady focus on history—the centuries that stamped African Americans with inferiority, the generations required to complete the struggle to erase that stamp. Yet more important, common sense does not confuse self-praise with self-exertion. It recognizes the difference between ceaselessly revisiting white America's midcentury advance to tolerance and working practically to mitigate the country's end-of-the-century race problems.

In the Civil Rights era the experience for many millions of Americans was one of discovery; a hitherto unimagined continent of human reality and history came into view, inducing genuine concern and self-forgetfulness. Minds were overwhelmed with consciousness of how shamefully wrong a wrong could be known to be by mere human beings, prisoners (usually) of moral labyrinths. The white majority was pushed toward direct engagement with facts of caste. At that particular moment, for that particular generation, the act of liking and admiring African Americans had some claim as morally creative; it entailed, for more than a few whites, a departure from local convention, even a degree of risk.

But that moment belongs to the distant past, and the practice of warping it into the present, as a permanently "current" event, would be farcical were its substantive social effect not cruel. Thirty and forty years after gestures of personal white-black amity stopped endangering anybody for a millisecond, the society continues to distract itself with new episodes of brave white dawnings, endless tales of formerly oblivious or heartless white persons who become civil, find astonishing pleasure in the company of an African American, and begin to *understand.* Now playing virtually nonstop in every medium, our national, self-congratulating epic of amity provides the right-minded with unlimited occasions for contemplating their own sensitive, antiracist selves— and no occasion whatever for confronting objective race realities. It also provides the majority culture with huge supplies of fantasy capital—fantasy moral capital. Each story of "improved" white attitudes qualifies as a contribution to solving the "black problem"—a daily deposit in a white goodness savings account.

Lately white leaders have been drawing ever more confidently on that account—the moral wealth accruing from dramatized versions of dogmas of black-white mutuality and sameness—to finance bold new enterprises in white exculpation and preceptorship. Figures of cultural influence speak and act as though a gulf has opened between white America and any lingering black troubles; the larger society learns from these figures that black choices alone now determine black fates and that the white majority's present and future role is merely to rebuke bad choices and applaud choices that are morally and socially life enhancing. Taking the pulpit in Dr. King's church, President Clinton chastises blacks for betraying King's heritage—failing to stand firm against crime and illegitimate pregnancy. The argument, namely that citizen-parents in a crime-ridden community must mobilize themselves against social disaster instead of feebly acceding to it, is unexceptionable. But the argument is couched in language that refuses any acknowledgment of the barriers against hope needing to be overcome. The near-explicit claim is that the minority, rendered free and equal by law and white fellow feeling, and offered unconditioned choices between social evil and social good by the majority, is perversely choosing evil.

Official preaching against black irresponsibility is accompanied by stern legislative and administrative initiatives—measures presented as a long overdue change of direction from coddling and permissiveness to punishment of willful black laziness and promiscuity. The message is that, while hatred may formerly have been an extenuating circumstance, today, with good feeling ascendant and black economic progress assured, nothing can excuse black misdeeds.

Friendship orthodoxy provides essential cover both for the sermonizing and for the emerging punitiveness. It establishes the spirit of amity as an all-pervasive force

guaranteeing that any seeming severity at this hour toward African Americans is quite unconnected with the
hostility and meanness that pollute our past. That guarantee certifies, for instance, that current mockery of
so-called political correctness is benign. Like contemporary tellers of friendship tales, PC baiters shrug off
historical injury to blacks as well as the evidence that
white America created the dysfunctional black bottom
caste; they lead the national chorus that presents African Americans as more or less universally middle
class—an omnipotent minority unfairly oppressing the
white working-class majority and causing constituted
authority of every sort (elected officials, university ad-
ministrators, teachers, publishers, advertisers) to trim
and tremble. Like tellers of friendship tales, PC baiters
avoid indictment as racist because their voices carry no
direct, personal animus toward blacks—and racism,
says friendship orthodoxy, is nothing other than direct,
personal animus.

Predictably the triumph of the orthodoxy has
forced those concerned about declining interest in the
black cause to fight back on the enemy's terms.
Caught in the web that friendship orthodoxy spins,
they find themselves denying that ill will has ended—
charging that hatred is still the white norm, accusing
mainstream whites of harboring vicious feelings. The
truth that demands to be told—that while the battle
against personal hatred has been won, the necessary

struggle for substantive racial development has only begun—becomes inexpressible.

Three decades ago the myth that some humans are more human than others, whites more human than blacks, was overturned; a new concept of black identity gained approval; the common human bond was affirmed. The next step seemed obvious: society would have to face up to the entailments of the common bond and acknowledge that, when one race deprives another of its humanity over centuries, the deprivers are obligated to aid in restoring the humanity of the deprived. Recognition of the common bond carried with it an imperative first alluded to, indistinctly, in *Brown v. Board of Education of Topeka*, that of mounting a comprehensive program of caste-dismantling development for the entire black population.

As early as 1966 the country took a significant step toward such a program. In a case brought in New Orleans, a federal court approved what James P. Turner, longtime career official in the Justice Department's Civil Rights Division, described as "the first-ever race-conscious remedy" of labor union denials, to blacks, of chances to learn and work in a trade. Other cases followed, in Philadelphia and elsewhere, breaking down patterns of exclusion and approving preferential treatment—affirmative action—for qualified blacks who applied for upper-tier educational and occupational places. Affirmative action policy constituted an ac-

Benjamin DeMott

knowledgment of job ceilings, as well as of other obstacles to black advancement; the policy signified awareness, at some level, that the nation had a caste problem.
Congress itself asserted as much when it passed a special economic stimulus package in 1979 in which 10
percent of a Public Works Act appropriation was set
aside for minority contractors.

That moment was a potential turning point. Pa-
tiently explained, justified, and promoted, the congressional action might have introduced America to its own
caste history, might have begun the serious schooling on
the subject necessary to build support for better conceived programs of development: programs flexible
enough to include, in time, appropriate means testing
(insurance, that is, against the bestowal of advantages
on rich blacks) yet adapted to the true magnitude of the
developmental task.

As is well known, that serious schooling didn't
occur. Within barely half a decade of the congressional
initiative, "preference" became the object of widespread public derision. The lines of attack were various.
Nonblack minorities denounced what was termed the
"legitimizing of quotas"—arrangements that Jews
among others remembered to have blocked their own
ascent. A black professional, Stephen Carter, wrote a
memoir reporting that the experience of benefiting from
affirmative action—life as "an affirmative action
baby"—was personally humiliating; he argued, not
without cause, that many of those whom the program

was meant to vault upward from nowhere in fact had belonged from birth to the middle class. Others held that affirmative action induced higher levels of color consciousness when the only proper goal was color blindness. Social critics observed that affirmative action visibly assaulted equality of opportunity—the key item in the pacifying mythology of the classless society.

Behind these and other complaints against affirmative action lay race pride, old-style race hostility, class guilt, sincere commitment to democratic values. None of the complaints was so unshakably anchored in logic as to be unanswerable. The complainants prevailed— the country inched toward recognition of the facts of its past only to turn away—because of the interaction of the movement from liberalism to neoconservatism, the emergence of a not negligible black middle class, and the influence of the dogmas of instant equality and mutuality studied in these chapters.

No list of abstract "causal factors" feels commensurate, to be sure, with the complex politico-cultural countercurrents and particularities of race history in the post–Civil Rights decades. Among some whites negative attitudes toward programs benefiting blacks were spurred by gang violence, the "drug culture," and urban riots. Some political leaders and "media influentials" found personal advantage in spreading falsehoods about both black work opportunities and levels of income support.

One myth held that mounting jobless rates among

blacks reflected mounting indolence. (The myth ignored the truth that, between 1972 and 1987, close to
15 million American workers—blacks disproportion-
ately represented among them—were directly affected
by the disappearance of low-wage, entry-level industrial jobs; official effort either at explaining the trend or
at mitigating its effects was minimal.) Another myth
held that, from the inception of the War on Poverty to
the present, levels of welfare and other support for the
black poor trended irreversibly upward. ("Between
1979 and 1986," Elliott Currie notes, attacking this
claim, "the average benefit under Aid to Families with
Dependent Children [AFDC] fell by about 20 percent in
real terms, while the proportion of poor children actually receiving benefits fell from 72 to 60 percent." In
1979, he adds, "about one poor family in five was
pulled above the poverty line by some combination of
AFDC, social security, and unemployment insurance:
but by 1986, just one in *nine.*")

The collapse of economic opportunity, outbreaks of
desperate black protest that infuriated the majority, political manipulation of "angry white males"—these
were but a few of the forces figuring in the full-scale
frontal assault, launched in the mid-1990s, on affirmative action (and on welfare and urban housing programs as well).

But the failure of educated, enlightened whites to
defend against the assault remains attributable, in no
small measure, to the influence of the dogmas of black-

white sameness that took hold under the aegis of friendship orthodoxy. Excited by the resurgence of the ideal of equality and by the heady discovery of black-white human solidarity, liberal wisdom in the immediate post–Civil Rights era commenced minimizing the impact of the black past—the conditions that made programs of development a necessity. Rearguard racist tirades on black "inferiority" were answered by right-minded whites with assertions, absolute and unqualified, of black-white equality—no acknowledgment of distance resulting from separate caste backgrounds, separate modes of education and training, separate ways of achieving selfhood, separate levels of economic resource. The assertions were strengthened by the national feeling for the social potency of openhanded, one-on-one warmth. "Personalizing" and sociability were in the American grain; programs of racewide development were not. "Getting to know one another" roused increasing enthusiasm; black identity underwent reconstruction: from subhuman to "just like us." Wishfulness—the kind borne in such slogans as we're all in the same boat, all taking our chances as we must—assumed command, undermining the ability of the fair-minded to grasp that "decent" denials of difference obliterated caste history and left the largest sector of African America utterly defenseless.

The weaknesses of official policy built on these denials will appear only when questioning and criticism have laid bare the flaws in its foundation. And the im-

pulse to question and criticize will stir only when right-
minded America recovers its clarity about black distance and black need. Four primary truths form the
basis for realistic policy: (1) black-white differences remain of large consequence; (2) the differences flow
from caste history; (3) the majority culture bears heavy
responsibility for the deficits stemming from these differences; (4) without broadscale programs of development, black advance will not continue, and the gap both
within the African American caste itself and between
whites and blacks generally will only worsen.

Progress toward policy built on these truths can't
be speeded by denunciation and excoriation. It is true
that well-meaning fantasies of black-white sameness
strengthen educated resistance to admitting truths of
white responsibility, true also that this resistance inten-
sifies the ultimately self-destructive oppositional mentality in bottom-caste blacks. But it matters deeply that
the fantasies are not, by and large, rooted in hatred. To
wish equality for blacks, to wish that the award of rights
meant the award of justice, to wish that the uncovering
of sameness under the skin could truly place blacks and
whites all in the same boat—these are not blameworthy
desires. They blend positives with negatives. They reflect, undeniably, eagerness to restage the moral drama
of majority-minority relations so that whites are no longer represented as oppressors—and opportunism and
sometimes cynicism are discernible in that eagerness.
But the desires also reflect the admirable American dis-

taste for hierarchical models of social life—a populism that surfaces as frequently in conservative as in liberal times.

For these reasons, white delusions that today threaten to impede black advance will not be swiftly cast off. And it bears repeating that those who undertake to awaken the majority to the nature of the delusions should not assume that high-toned hectoring or indictment will be effective. White Americans won't be shamed out of the fantasy into which they have fallen; they will have to be reasoned into abandoning it.

To strong supporters of the black struggle for equality, this book's absorption with majority thought and feeling has doubtless come to seem, long before now, an act of truancy. Past contributors to that struggle didn't sweat the job of understanding majority attitudes. They bent to the work of documenting objective horror and injustice, dramatizing the truth of injury and relying on the fair-minded to cry out in protest. The barrier to the crusade for equality was the heedlessness, among the well off and well meaning, of black suffering. The task was to attack that heedlessness, and activists succeeded brilliantly at it, pushing the majority—as I said—toward self-forgetfulness and realistic engagement with facts of caste.

But the movement at this hour, as the body of evidence surveyed here suggests, is in the opposite direction—toward self-sentimentalization and descent into obscurantism. Periodically an urban convulsion interrupts the descent, but such interruptions aren't long-lived. The personalizing, moralizing, miniaturizing habit of thought reasserts itself. After the Los Angeles riots in 1992, a police chief, a jury, a suburb, even an earlier presidential administration were demonized. (Observers remarked, with an air of trenchancy, that Simi Valley, home of violent police officers, was also the home of the Ronald Reagan library.) Enlightened whites found themselves buried once again beneath heartening images of their sympathy and of the essential sameness-under-the-skin of the races. Fundamentals quickly disappeared.

Those well acquainted with this pattern of events— those fearing yet another betrayal of black America— can no longer give themselves solely to rousing anger at objective inequities or to indicting the cruel and oblivious. They must pursue knowledge of the unexamined orthodoxy—race thinking in communities unconscious of animus, patterns of perception which, within the right-minded majority culture, transform outrage at injustice into evil and apathy into good, processes by which seemingly unrelated elements (pop sentiment, economic statistics at once correct and misleading, accredited middlebrow moralizing, pseudohistory, can-do mythology, and the rest) have been fashioned into the internally consistent yet at bottom false account of the nation's race problems now passing current as "sound."

I would add here at the end that the knowledge I speak of—solid understanding of the defects of false accounts of our race problems—benefits whites as well as blacks. Even as the mind-set these pages have anatomized visits immeasurable harm on the nation's largest minority, it does damage to the majority, desensitizing perception, diminishing the feeling for social existence as it is, misrepresenting inevitabilities as surprises, and exacting assent to an array of plausible-appearing absurdities. To mention this isn't to place losses of acuity by the privileged on an equal footing with pain suffered by the minority. The point is simply that, for citizens white and black persuaded of their personal stake in the future of reason, studying friendship orthodoxy, and disputing and overturning it, is best understood as an act not of compassion but of self-interest.

Acknowledgments

This book has roots in West Point, Mississippi; years ago, when Marian Wright Edelman was Marian Wright, barely out of college, she made it possible for me (and several others) to work in a tutorial project for African American children at Mary Holmes Junior College in that embattled town. Later, in Washington, DC, in the 1970s, my teachers were the poets Lucille Clifton and Sam Cornish; we were co-workers in a teaching program in the district public schools. A major contribution came from colleagues at Bethune-Cookman College, especially Margaret Williams, who not only took me in as a visiting faculty member for parts of two years in the mid-1980s but time and again set me straight—gently—when I misread my students' thinking. The people I mention are responsible not for this book's argument but for the gradual growth of my confidence that I was *capable* of grasping an important truth about black-white relationships.

My friends Donald Bigelow, Eric McKitrick, Richard Todd, and Alan Williams counseled me generously and wisely; I had invaluable guidance from Phyllis Westberg and Anton Mueller; Joseph Ellis put his own research aside to answer my questions; Greg Gallagher at the Century Library and the members of the reference staff of the Frost Library at Amherst were generous as well as efficient.

My children—they are in their thirties and forties with independent careers—were involved in this work from the start, bringing to bear their unique, intensely relevant experience, clarifying the drift, thinking and arguing through its stages. Midway, events obliged them to interrupt their lives to help keep the author's body as well as book in one piece. The debt I owe them and their mates and their mother—my wife, Peggy Craig DeMott—lies far beyond words.

Notes

Introduction

other Americans. Steele's extended discussions of immigrant groups, in *The Content of Our Character* (1990), occur in chaps. 4 and 9 ("The Recomposed Self" and "The Memory of Enemies" in HarperPerennial ed., 1991).

Jesse Jackson continues to call: See Yolanda Woodlee, "Clinton Urged to Give D.C. Recreation Programs a Boost," *Washington Post*, March 4, 1994, sec. D, p. 3, and Janita Poe, "Jackson Tells PUSH America

Must Rebuild," *Chicago Tribune*, September 28, 1992, sec. 2C, p. 2.

John E. Jacob advocates: See John E. Jacob, "America's Cities Need an Urban Marshall Plan," *USA Today*, vol. 119 (March 1991), pp. 34–36.

Henry Louis Gates combines his call: See Gates, "Two nations . . . both black," *Forbes*, vol. 150 (September 14, 1992), pp. 132–38.

Recent all-black panel discussions: see Bob Herbert, "Who Will Help the Black Man?" *New York Times Magazine*, December 4, 1994, pp. 72–77, and "Forum on the Responsibility of Intellectuals," *Boston Review*, vol. 18, no. 1 (January–February 1993), pp. 22–28.

beauty within." The song title is "We Shall Be Free."

1. Visions of Black-White Friendship

leaders rafting. See "Two in Gang Return from Trip with Brown," *New York Times*, May 15, 1992, p. 17.

any differently." Gwen Ifil, "Clinton Blames Bush and Republicans for Racial Turmoil," *New York Times*, May 3, 1992, p. 28.

dome-headed twins. Like every aspect of interracial relations in the United States, the purposeful blurring of racial identity has a complex history. *Dark Twins: Imposture and Identity in Mark Twain's America* (Chicago: Chicago U.P., 1989), by Susan Gillman, studies one memorable moment in that past.

American way.") Jannette L. Dates, "Commercial Television," in Jannette L. Dates and William Barlow, eds., *Split Image: African Americans in the Mass Media* (Washington: Howard U. P., 1990), p. 274.

"Everlasting friendship." John Guare, *Six Degrees of Separation* (New York: Random House, 1990), p. 99. Subsequent quotations from the play are from this text.

white children). See Andrew Hacker, *Two Nations* (New York: Scribner, 1992), pp. 98–100.

2. The Mystique of Sympathy

Affirmative Civility." Studs Terkel, *Race* (New York: New Press, 1992), pp. 17–18.

public sphere. At moments in *Race* Terkel speaks to issues in public policy, but his principal concerns lie elsewhere. Micaela DiLeonardo assesses the book justly in "Boyz on the Hood," *The Nation*, August 17–24, 1992, p. 178.

their home. Roger Rosenblatt, "Carefully Taught," *Family Circle*, February 18, 1992, p. 152. Subsequent quotations are from this text.

14 percent. Black income, poverty, and net worth statistics quoted here and below are taken from Census Bureau reports and from Andrew Hacker's *Two Nations* (New York: Scribner, 1992). See chap. 6, "The Real Income Gap" and "Statistical Sources" (pp. 93–106, 223–236). Hacker has been sharply criticized for writing skeptically about the alleged vast expansion of the "black middle class" and about black economic advance in general. See Orlando Patterson and Chris Winship, "White Poor, Black Poor," *New York Times*, May 3, 1992, sec. 4, p. 17.

as among whites. U. S. Public Health figures quoted by Andrew Hacker in "The Blacks and Clinton," *New York Review*, January 28, 1993, p. 14.

than that of whites. See *Statistical Record of Black America*, ed. Carrell Peterson Horton and Jessie Carney Smith (Detroit: Gale, 1990), p. 400.

ever were." John Updike, "A Letter to My Grandsons," *Self-Consciousness* (New York: Knopf, 1989), p. 195. Subsequent quotations are from this text.

and programs." James Alan McPherson, "Out of Many, a Few," *Reconstruction*, vol. 1, no. 3 (1991), 87. Subsequent quotations are from this text.

3. Because We Like Them

and Customers." Wal-Mart circular, Montgomery, AL, June 1992, p. 6. Subsequent quotations are from this text.

Desert Storm." AT&T ad, *City Sun* (NY), May 15–21, 1991, p. 38.

naval heroes. Chrysler ad, *City Sun* (NY), February 6–12, 1991, p. 2.

your business." Manufacturers Hanover ad, *City Sun* (NY), October 31–November 6, 1990, p. 22.

Because Con Ed likes them: Con Edison ad, *City Sun* (NY), February 13, 1991, p. 13.

black youngsters). Coca-Cola ad, *City Sun* (NY), February 13–19, 1991, p. 42.

the country." Reebok ad, *City Sun* (NY), October 31–November 6, 1990, p. 49.

to listen") IBM ad, *New Yorker,* December 23, 1991, p. 9.

our hearts." Brooklyn Union Gas ad, *City Sun* (NY), February 13–19, 1991, p. 7.

and *Kindness*"). RJReynolds ad, *City Sun* (NY), January 9–15, 1991, p. 2.

American Express focuses: the ad, copyright 1992 American Express Travel Related Services Company Inc., ran in *The New Yorker* and other upscale print media.

people, too." *People* ad in *Sports Illustrated,* January 15, 1992, p. 1.

the game). See Ellen Goodman, "In L.A., No More American Dream," *Daily Hampshire Gazette* (Northampton, MA), August 7, 1992, p. 8.

gone up!"). Leslie Savon, "Op Ad," *Village Voice,* November 13, 1990, p. 52.

attention, please?"). *TV Guide,* October 26, 1990, p. 19.

about them." Richard Reeves, "Boyz' Is Interesting Foreign Film," *Montgomery Advertiser,* July 31, 1991, p. 10A.

with them." See Michael Massing's discussion of Kotlowitz and Frey in "Ghetto Blasting," *New Yorker,* January 16, 1995, p. 32.

not prejudiced." Daniel Pinkwater, *Lizard Music* (1976), quoted by Albert Williams, "Victor in Wonderland," *Chicago Reader*, May 1, 1992, p. 36.

toward blacks. Michael Musto, "La Dolce Musto," *Village Voice*, February 19, 1991, p. 44.

is confused." Rob Tannenbaum, "Little Bit o' Soul," *Village Voice*, May 12, 1992, p. 72.

= Brown." Joe Wood, "Cultural Consumption, from Elvis Presley to the Young Black Teenagers," *Voice Rock & Roll Quarterly*, March 1991, p. 11.

is silly." Leslie Savon, "Op Ad," *Village Voice*, May 26, 1992, p. 54.

the globe. Ibid.

"Dat's his natchal odor."): See *Laugh and Let Laugh*, by Grandma (Talladega: Roberts & Son, 1953), p. 49.

aren't insincere. "Whatever the continuing dilemmas of race in the United States," writes Thomas Bender, "no one can go back. Black humanity has become obvious, and affairs can no longer be imagined otherwise. In the cultural mainstream, the vocabulary to deny black humanity is no longer available." See "Sensationalism and the New York Press," by John D. Stevens with remarks by Thomas Bender (New York: Freedom Forum Media Studies Center, 1991), p. 14.

humanizing influence. Philip Fisher argues—in *Hard Facts: Setting and Form in the American Novel* (New York: Oxford U.P., 1985)—that, for white America, Harriet Beecher Stowe's *Uncle Tom's Cabin* virtually *created* black people as human beings. The standard work on the history of humanizing and dehumanizing images of blacks is George M. Fredrickson's *The Black Image in the White Mind: The Debate on Afro-American Character and Destiny, 1817–1914* (New York: Harper and Row, 1971). A way of gauging the progress is to view friendship motifs in the light of the objection by individual blacks (voiced by writers from W. E. B. Du Bois to James Baldwin) to being perceived as a "problem" or "strange experience," never simply as persons. See Ross Posnock, "Black Intellectuals Past and Present," *Raritan Quarterly*, Winter 1993, p. 135.

racial identity"). Jon Michael Spencer, "Trends of Opposition to Multiculturalism," *Black Scholar*, Winter–Spring 1993, quoted by Lawrence Wright, in "One Drop of Blood," *New Yorker*, July 25, 1994, p. 55. See also Ivan Hannaford, "The Idiocy of Race," *Wilson Quarterly*, Spring 1994, p. 8. Contemporary thought on these matters is indirectly but deeply indebted to the landmark twentieth-century works—Edward Said's *Orientalism*, for one—clarifying the social construction of identity: "sameness," "difference," cultural boundaries in general.

4. Caste Society/Opportunity Society (I)

above \$35,000. For a full account of patterns of black earnings, see Andrew Hacker, *Two Nations* (New York: Scribner, 1992), chap. 6 ("The Racial Income Gap").

as extraordinary. Over the past quarter century social scientists have produced an impressive body of studies bearing on caste and stratification in America. (The subjects include stereotyping, vulnerability to stereotypes, alienation from achievement or "disidentification," and performance anxiety.) Much of this work has concentrated on schooling problems of minority students—and on the shaping of these problems by the interaction of structural factors with cultural and psychological factors.

My aim is to widen the nonacademic audience for the general themes and perspectives of this research, and toward that end I focus on the pioneering studies of the scholar—John U. Ogbu—to whom researchers in these fields acknowledge greatest indebtedness. Among the more interesting current research bearing on Ogbu's arguments and insights is that of Mary C. Waters, Loeb professor of sociology at Harvard, and that of Claude M. Steele, professor of psychology at Stanford. Waters's work centers on black immigrants and native-born African Americans in New York City (see Mary C. Waters, "The Role of Lineage in Identity Formation Among Black Americans," *Qualitative Sociology*, Spring 1991, p. 57). Steele's subject is "Race and the Schooling of Black Americans" (an article of his under that title, addressed to general readers, appeared in *The Atlantic* of April 1992). See also James W. Stigler, Richard A. Schweder, and Gilbert Herdt, eds., *Cultural Psychology: Essays on Comparative Human Development*

(New York: Cambridge U. P., 1990), and Kofi Lomotey, *Going to School: The African American Experience*, Frontiers in Education Series (Albany: State U. of New York P., 1990).

caste society.'' Kenneth Keniston, "Foreword," in John U. Ogbu, *Minority Education and Caste* (New York: Academic Press, 1978), p. xiii.

American Dilemma.'') Ibid.

"way of life.'' Myron Magnet, "America's Underclass: What to Do?" *Fortune*, May 11, 1987, p. 130, quoted by Michael Katz in *The Undeserving Poor* (New York: Pantheon, 1989), p. 198. Katz and Adolph Reed are the most persuasive recent critics of the concept of the underclass; they indict it for representing poverty as the result of bad behavior and bad values. "If we say that poor people are poor because they have bad values," writes Adolph Reed, "we let government off the hook, even though conscious government policy—for example, in the relations between support for metropolitan real estate speculation and increasing homelessness, malnutrition, and infant mortality—is directly implicated in causing poverty" ("The Underclass Myth," *Progressive*, August 1991, p. 20). See also Reed's "Parting the Waters," a review-essay on recent work treating the "coexistence of racial and class oppression" (*Nation*, November 23, 1992, p. 633). For research support of these arguments, see Marta Tienda and Haya Stier, "Joblessness and Shiftlessness: Labor Force Activity in Chicago's Inner City," in Christopher

Jencks and Paul Peterson, eds., *The Urban Underclass* (Washington, DC: Brookings, 1991), p. 135, and Marta Tienda, "Poor People, Poor Places: Deciphering Neighborhood Effects on Poverty Outcomes," in Joan Huber, ed., *Macro-Micro Linkages in Sociology* (Newbury Park, CA: Sage, 1991), p. 244.

[maladjusted] individuals." Ogbu, *Minority Education*, p. 102.

undesirable work. The following discussion of black access to education and jobs is based on Ogbu's *Minority Education* (chaps. 4 and 5, "Black Access to Education" and "The Job Ceiling and Other Barriers," pp. 101–147, 149–176).

mass consumed." Ogbu, *Minority Education*, p. 345.

minority group." Ibid.

common elements. The following discussion of caste and caste-dismantling efforts in foreign societies is based on Ogbu's six cross-cultural studies in *Minority Education* (chaps. 8–13, pp. 241–342). Page references for quotations are as follows: *"polluting"* (308), *"black ones"* (333), *"washermen, and laborers"* (288), *"lazy, improvident"* (268), *"imagination deficiency"* (278), *"educational needs"* (254), *"Maori community"* (283), *"protective discrimination"* (301), *"cognitive development"* (338), *"in school"* (284), *"help them"* (262), *"private schools"* (298), *"own ability"* (296), *"or Mongoloids"* (252), *"mental capacity"* (333), *"of untouchability"* (296), *"Buraku problem"* (316), *"been given"*

(352); *"American schools"* (319), *"status per se"* (320), *"other means"* (320).

5. Caste Society/Opportunity Society (II)

the planters." John U. Ogbu, *Minority Education and Caste* (New York: Academic Press, 1978), p. 110.

remained unshaken. For discussions of Walker's, Douglass's and Delany's comments on majority morality, see Vincent Harding's *There Is a River: The Black Struggle for Freedom in America* (New York: Harcourt Brace, 1981), pp. 86–96, 172.

(In South Central Los Angeles: See Barbara Vobejda and William Casey, "Los Angeles Swept by Decade of Social, Economic Change," *Washington Post*, May 11, 1992, sec. A, p. 1, and Michele L. Norris, "Among L.A.'s Biggest Losses: Jobs," *Washington Post*, May 13, 1992, sec. A, p. 1. For an update on Los Angeles unemployment and related factors, see Frederick Rose, "Los Angeles Still Awaits Social, Economic Renewal," *Wall Street Journal*, April 19, 1993, sec. A, p. 4.

you say.' " James P. Comer, "Educating Poor Minority Children," *Scientific American*, 259 (November 1988), p. 46.

"opportunity aversion." The phrase is Shelby Steele's. See chapter 11 for an extended discussion of Steele's *The Content of Our Character* (1990).

sympathies lie. Some important academic and journalistic critiques of *The Bell Curve* are collected in

The Bell Curve Wars, ed. Steven Fraser (New York: Basic, 1995).

over generations. Others beside caste theorists have been insightful, of course, about the range of those effects. See, for example, David Kirp, *Just Schools: The Idea of Racial Equality in American Education* (Berkeley: U. of California P., 1982).

individualistic competitiveness" . . . "manipulation." Ogbu, *Minority Education,* p. 198.

token reward." Ibid., p. 199. Ogbu is quoting a 1970 Social Science Research Council paper, by William A. Shack, "On Black American Values in White America."

American identity." John U. Ogbu, "Minority Status and Literacy in Comparative Perspective," *Daedalus,* vol. 119, no. 2 (1990, Special Issue: "Literacy in America"), p. 154, and "Cultural Boundries and Minority Youth Orientation Towards Work Preparation," in *Adolescence and Work: Influences of Social Structure, Markets and Culture,* ed. D. Stern and D. Eichorn (Hillsdale, NJ: Lawrence Erlbaum Associates, 1989), p. 110. Subsequent quotations in this paragraph are from these texts. See also Ogbu's essay "On Academic Underperformance and Dropping Out Among Involuntary Minorities," in *Dropouts from School: Issues, Dilemmas, and Solutions,* ed. Lois Weis, Eleanor Farrar, and Hugh L. Petrie (Albany: SUNY Press, 1989), pp. 181–204.

by the mainstream." James Comer, "Educating

Poor Minority Children," p. 46. Subsequent quotations in this paragraph are from this article.

white community." Ogbu, "On Academic Underperformance," p. 181.

"Unlike the caste groups": Ogbu, *Minority Education*, p. 24.

6. Caste Society/Opportunity Society (III)

his 'progress.'" John U. Ogbu, *Minority Education and Caste* (New York: Academic Press, 1978), p. 135.

rational grounds. Evaluation anxiety has haunted Head Start from its inception. William Ayer writes in *The Nation* (February 1, 1993) that "the idea of a 'comprehensive child development program' seemed unnecessarily complex, and the 'Johnsons [LBJ and Lady Bird] and other promoters . . . found it simpler just to talk about I.Q. scores.' [Sargent] Shriver told his staff in 1965 to 'prove' the value of Head Start by finding out 'how many IQ points are gained for every dollar invested,' and in 1966, in Congressional testimony, he falsely claimed that Head Start 'had had great impact on children—in terms of raising IQs, as much as 8 to 10 IQ points in a six-week period.' Lyndon Johnson alleged, when he received the Second Report of the President's Panel on Mental Retardation in 1968, that 'Project Head Start, which only began in 1965, has actually raised the IQ of hundreds of thousands of children in this country.' " Ayer's quotations are from

Head Start: The Inside Story of America's Most Successful Educational Experiment, by Edward Zigler and Susan Muenchow (New York: Basic, 1993).

before the general public. Comer reflects at length on "social development schools" in his book *School Power: Implications of an Intervention Project* (New York: Free Press, 1980).

Comer notes that bottom-caste parents: see "Educating Poor Minority Children," p. 46.

[black] Americans." See William Finnegan, "A Street Kid in the Drug Trade, Part II," *New Yorker*, September 17, 1990, p. 66.

7. Invisible Woman

four days. My account of the Joyce Ann Moore trial is based on videotapes supplied by the Video Library Service of The American Lawyer/Courtroom Television Network.

8. Chicken George & Co. Versus History

it done." Taylor Branch quotes the Moses speech in *Parting the Waters: America in the King Years* (New York: Simon and Schuster, 1989), p. 733.

political grounds." David R. Roediger, *The Wages of Whiteness* (New York: Verso, 1991), p. 31.

caste theorists. Vincent Harding brings the insurrections and revolts to life in *There Is a River* (New York: Harcourt Brace, 1981). Eugene D. Genovese's *Roll, Jordan, Roll* (New York: Pantheon, 1974) remains authoritative on differences between Old South slave revolts and those in the Caribbean and Brazil. Houston A. Baker's studies of the African American "vernacular" document numerous modes of cultural resistance— from slave narratives to the blues, "signifying" to Black English. See also Roger Abrahams's *Singing the Master* (New York: Pantheon, 1992), a folklorist's striking inquiry into "active resistance," by slaves, through the maintenance of "alternative perspectives toward time, work, and status" (p. xxii).

American Individualism. Information about the production and audience of *Roots* is drawn from Leslie Fishbein, " 'Roots:' Docudrama and the Interpretation of History," in *American History/American Television*, ed. John E. O'Connor (New York: Ungar, 1983). The intricate theoretical matters that figure in academic discussion of "dramatized history" are treated by several hands in *Revisioning History: Film and the Construction of a New Past*, ed. Robert Rosenstone (Princeton: Princeton U. P., 1995).

the other." See Fishbein, "Roots," p. 290.

its institutions." Eric Foner, article in *Sevendays* (March 1977), quoted by Fishbein, pp. 300–01.

to accrue). "The very notion of America's exceptionalism—the 'American Dream' of a land of promise . . .—was originally made possible by the availability of cheap, coerced labor to clear and cultivate the most fertile lands and to produce export crops for which there was seemingly an unlimited demand. From the early

West India trade of the northeastern colonies to the cotton exports that helped pay for northern railroads and industrialization, America's economy depended largely on slave labor" (David Brion Davis, "The American Dilemma," *New York Review of Books,* July 16, 1992, p. 14).

9. The Issueless War and the Movement That Never Was

"morally bankrupt." Jeanie Attie, "Illusions of History: A Review of *The Civil War,*" *Radical History,* Winter 1992, pp. 98, 102.

it covers." Ibid., p. 97.

Are blacks, he asked, "on a par with ourselves?": See Jefferson's letter to John Holmes (April 22, 1820) in *The Works of Thomas Jefferson,* ed. Paul Leicester Ford (New York: Putnam, 1904–05), vol. 10, p. 157. Also see Jefferson's *Notes on the State of Virginia,* Query XIV, in *Writings* (New York: Library of America, 1984), pp. 256–75.

the South." Daniel Boorstin, *Hidden History: Exploring Our Secret Past* (New York: Vintage, 1989), p. 173. James M. McPherson stresses the same point: "By the generation before the Civil War most white southerners—and a good many northerners as well—not only considered liberty and slavery quite compatible, but even believed that the slavery of blacks was essential to the liberty of whites." See James M. McPherson, *Abra-*

ham Lincoln and the Second American Revolution (New York: Oxford U. P., 1991), p. 48.

rights workers.") See Harvard Sitkoff, *The Struggle for Black Equality* (New York: Hill and Wang, 1981), p. 177.

10. Clearing the Conscience (I)

pass unscathed." Alfred Kazin, "Cry, the Beloved Country," *Forbes*, September 14, 1992, p. 150.

to do." "The Quiz," *New York Times*, January 5, 1992 (sec. 4A, "Education Life,"), p. 14. Page numbers for quotations from this section are as follows: *"a handout"* (18), *"on a farm"* (18), *"in school"* (21), *"can't do"* (8), *"age four"* (22), *"top colleges"* (28), *"to them"* (22), *"of place"* (23), *well-off parents* (30–31), *"six weeks"* (41), *"public schools"* (35).

Gibson recalls." James Moffett, *Storm in the Mountains* (Carbondale: Southern Illinois U. P., 1988), p. 137.

Stay in School seem[s]": see Anthony Carter Paige, "David May Not Be Stern, but He Gets the Job Done," *City Sun*, July 30–August 6, 1991, p. 32.

11. Clearing the Conscience (II)

this out." The character functions as a spokesperson of a sort for Spike Lee. "All I'm saying," Lee told one interviewer, "is that black people haven't really thought of owning businesses." *Rolling Stone*, July 11–25, 1991, p. 64.

the like. In *Do the Right Thing* Lee himself briefly opens up the ambiguities of "friendship" in exchanges between one point-of-view character, Mookie, and Pino, son of the proprietor of Sal's Famous Pizzeria. Pino is, simultaneously, a racist and a Magic Johnson and Eddie Murphy fan. This "sounds funny to me," Mookie tells Pino. "As much as you say nigger this and nigger that, all your favorite people are 'niggers.' " The inarticulate Pino responds: "It's different."

the hog."). "With Bob Grant, It's Not Chicken Talk," *New York Times*, October 27, 1994, p. B8.

in prison."). AP dispatch, "In Second Debate, Weld Strikes Back at Opponent," *Daily Hampshire Gazette* (Northampton, MA), October 27, 1994, p. 9.

not have." Laurie Loisel, "A Sampling of Itzkoff's Views," *Daily Hampshire Gazette*, October 27, 1994, p. 12.

Shelby Steele's." Will's blurb appears on the cover of *The Content of Our Character* (HarperPerennial ed., 1991).

without texts). See Jonathan Kozol, *Savage Inequalities* (New York: Crown, 1991), p. 110.

pursue power." Steele, *Content of Our Character*, p. 5. Page references for quotations from this book in this chapter are as follows: *"Howard Beach"* (15), *"to power"* (17), *"racial specifics"* (xi), *"uncomprehend-*

ingly reverential" (142), *"bettering themselves"* (17), *"admit it"* (23), *"our victimization"* (68), *"party line"* (72), *"denial . . . distortion"* (57–59), *"insistent way . . . her racism"* (58–59), *"black life"* (59), *"integration shock . . . responsible for them"* (60), *"anti-self . . . quietly to rest"* (55), *"We can talk . . . and power"* (28), *"Southeast Asia"* (69), *"delayed gratification"* (69), *"racial victimization"* (69), *"apply yourself"* (51), *"own lives"* (34), *"The responsible . . . has power"* (33–34).

compassionate ways.) Stephen L. Carter, *Reflections of an Affirmative Action Baby* (New York: Basic, 1991), p. 107.

"developmental assistance." Steele, *Content of Our Character,* pp. 91, 111–125. In interviews Steele often calls simultaneously for self-help and government help. "We need government intervention to help us," he told *Time* (August 12, 1991, p. 6). "But we've also got to help ourselves." And he continues to speak out both against "entitlements" and for "rights guaranteed to individuals and developmental help to those in need." See "How to Grow a Farrakhan," in *Journal of Blacks in Higher Education,* Spring 1994, p. 84.

12. Clearing the Conscience (II)

a trade. James P. Turner, "The Fairest Cure We Have," *New York Times,* April 16, 1995, p. 11.

middle class. See Stephen L. Carter, *Reflections of*

an Affirmative Action Baby (New York: Basic, 1991), p. 72: "The benefits of affirmative action fall to those least in need of them."

was minimal.). See Elliot Currie, *Reckoning: Drugs, the Cities, and the American Future* (New York: Hill and Wang, 1993), p. 130.

one in nine." Ibid., p. 134.

in hatred. "Because of its experience of cruel, centuries-long ill treatment," Nathan Glazer writes, one immigrant group—blacks—"is not yet fully incorporated in [the] generally successful process of nation-building. Present-day multiculturalism is a product of that apartness. Most of those who embrace it, I believe do so in the hope that it will overcome that apartness. They want, in some key respects, to become more like other Americans—for example, in educational achievement—not different from them, and believe that the way to becoming more like them is to take more account of difference, and yes, of ill-treatment, of past and current achievement, even if exaggerated." See "In Defense of Multiculturalism," *New Republic*, September 2, 1991, p. 22.

of truancy. Adolph Reed complains bitterly and penetratingly about the preoccupation of the public forum with "a discourse on how white people think about black people and how black people supposedly feel about it, buttressing a suspicion that this is all most whites care much about anyway." See "Tokens of the White Left," *Progressive*, December 1993, p. 20.